WRITING WORKSHOP
Paragraph and Sentence Practice

Joyce Pagurek
Carleton University

NEWBURY HOUSE PUBLISHERS
A division of HarperCollins*Publishers*

Library of Congress Cataloging in Publication Data

Pagurek, Joyce.
   Writing workshop.

   1. English language--Text-books for foreign speakers.
2. English language—Rhetoric. I. Title.
PE1128.P235   1984   808'.042   83-22095
ISBN 0-88377-405-4

NEWBURY HOUSE PUBLISHERS
A division of HarperCollins*Publishers*

Language Science
Language Teaching
Language Learning

Copyright © 1984 by Newbury House Publishers, Inc. All rights reserved. No part of this book may be reproduced or transmitted in any form or by any means, electronic or mechanical, including photocopying, recording, or by any information storage and retrieval system, without permission in writing from the Publisher.

Printed in the U.S.A.

First printing: February 1984
4 5 6 7 8 9 10 11

To
Lynne Young
for sharing her enthusiasm and love of ideas

ACKNOWLEDGMENTS

I am grateful to the teachers in the English Language Program, Carleton University, who field-tested the units and offered suggestions and advice: Lynne Young, Elizabeth Taborek, Pat Pappas, and Barbara Sandilands.

Thanks to Barbara Sandilands and Elizabeth Taborek for permission to use the topics in Exercise 1, Chapter 8, Cause 4,

I would especially like to thank Brigid Fitzgerald, whose encouragement, thoughtful comments, and practical suggestions have been invaluable.

Finally, thanks to Cheryl Pagurek whose sketches were the basis for the drawings in Chapters 4, 5, and 7.

J. L. P.

TO THE TEACHER

OBJECTIVES

The purpose of *Writing Workshop* is to teach students to write short pieces of coherent and cohesive discourse appropriate for a particular audience and purpose. It teaches the student to write longer, tighter sentences and better-organized paragraphs.

ORGANIZATION

Writing Workshop has ten chapters. The first presents the basic ideas of the text:
1. There is a functional relationship between sentences. These relationships are signaled by words called discourse markers. Discourse markers familiar to the student (*and, but, so*) are used to introduce the concept of functional relationships.
2. Paragraphs are groups of related sentences dealing with one topic. Concerns such as audience, purpose, topic sentence, support, concluding sentence, and organization of content are introduced.

In each of Chapters 2 through 9 a different organizational pattern is considered: generalization and support, enumeration, comparison, definition, cause and result, and static description. On the whole, these chapters are divided into three parts: Sentences, Paragraphs, and Exam-Type Questions. The latter section shows how the pattern taught in the chapter can be used to answer certain types of examination questions. Chapter 10 is a consolidation unit. Students are given information, an audience, and a purpose for writing. They must select appropriate patterns to organize each set of facts.

SPECIAL FEATURES

Integration of Skills

Although the focus of the book is writing, the other skills are integrated. For example, in order to gather data for their writing, students engage in either reading or speaking/listening activities. The questions on the model paragraph give students practice in both discourse analysis and note-taking.

Topics

There is a wide scope of topics to stimulate students' interest. Those of contemporary concern include subjects such as the environment (nuclear waste disposal; air, water, and noise pollution), computers and society, the economy (inflation, unemployment), and sociological changes (divorce, violence in cities, feminism). Students can also choose to write about their own experience if they select topics such as their country's customs, history, politics, or education system.

Sources of Information

The data for writing come from a variety of sources—graphics (charts and graphs), letters to the editor, minutes of and notes for meetings, travel brochures, advertisements, tables of consumer information on a variety of products, as well as class and group discussions of specific problems or subjects.

Contextualization

Paragraph writing never occurs in a vacuum. Students are given a perspective from which to write, an audience for whom to write, and a purpose. Some of the perspectives included are that of a journalist, an administrator, an economic or political analyst, a science or history textbook writer, or a student. The audiences aimed at are readers of different sections of a newspaper or magazine, a newspaper editor, textbook readers, business associates (e.g., a finance committee, a city council). The purpose for writing may be to inform, express opinion, compare, contrast, explain causes or results, recommend, or describe.

ACTIVITIES

In the first two parts of each chapter activities move from guided to open-ended.

Sentences

Introductory Activity: This is an activity which generates information for the student to write about in the exercises which follow. Examples of such activities are class or group discussions, making a survey, or extracting information from advertisements.

Presentation of Discourse Markers: The discourse markers for the unit are presented clearly in special type. They are divided into two groups:

GROUP A—This group contains coordinators, subordinators, and adverbial connectives. These discourse markers link sentences as well as express the functional relationship between the sentences.

GROUP B—This group of markers consists of other parts of speech (noun, preposition, determiner, verb phrase etc.). These markers do not link sentences grammatically. They have grammatical roles *within their own sentences* and also express functional relationships in these sentences (or, in some cases, with preceding ones).

Using Discourse Markers: These exercises provide (1) examples of how the discourse markers are used and (2) practice in using the discourse markers.

Guided Sentence Writing: Exercises such as sentence completion and sentence combining are included here. Guidance is given in varying degrees. For example, in the most guided activity students are given the sentences and the kind of discourse marker to use. Students are responsible only for providing the appropriate marker. In a less guided activity they are given the sentences; they must decide on the functional relationship between them and then provide the appropriate marker. In a still less guided activity, students are given information (in the form of a chart, table, ad, etc.) and a functional relationship (e.g., contrast). They are responsible for both composing the sentences and choosing an appropriate marker from Group A or B discourse markers. Not all these guided sentence activities are included in each unit. A selection from these is made, depending on what is most suitable for the particular unit.

Write Your Own Sentences: The final activity in the first part of the chapters is free sentence writing. Students provide their own content and choose the appropriate discourse markers from those they have learned in the unit.

Paragraphs

Read and Analyze: A piece of discourse which illustrates the organizational pattern of the unit is presented. Several types of writing are represented: letters, memos, excerpts from newspaper or magazine articles. Analysis of the paragraph focuses on the topic sentence, support, concluding sentence, discourse markers, audience, and purpose. This kind of analysis helps students with their reading as well as with their writing because they become more aware of how facts and ideas are organized in English. In addition, they gain some experience in note making as they fill in outlines based on the content of the paragraphs they have read.

Paragraph Format: The organizational pattern for the unit is presented in diagram form.

Class Composition: This is a guided group activity. The purpose is to allow the teacher to guide the class as a whole in the first attempt at a paragraph written according to the suggested pattern. Information for the paragraph arises from class discussion of a problem or of data in a chart or table. Audience, purpose, and suggestions for the content of topic and concluding sentences are provided. The paragraph is recorded on the board as it develops, and alternative ways of expressing ideas are discussed.

Guided Writing: This activity is similar to the class composition in the degree of guidance; however, here students work alone. They choose one of two topics for which written data are provided. The student is responsible for extracting the relevant information and writing about it, using the organization taught in the unit.

Write Your Own Paragraph: In this activity, students work alone. They are responsible for both the content and organization of their paragraphs. They can either choose their own topic, audience, and purpose or select one of several topics provided (each with its accompanying audience and purpose).

Exam-Type Questions

Students are shown how to use the organizational pattern taught in the unit to answer certain types of examination questions. Since this section will be most relevant if students work on questions based on their own studies or drawn from their reading program, the Teachers' Notes provide examples of different types of questions and guidance in formulating such questions based on a reading passage.

HOW TO USE THIS BOOK

Before starting a chapter, check the Teachers' Notes for explanations and/or suggestions. Feel free to adapt sections of this text so that the needs of particular groups of students are met more directly. This can be accomplished in a number of ways.

1. *Substitute topics* relevant to your students and use these for discussion and as a basis for writing.
2. After completing Chapters 1 and 2, *sequence the chapters* so that the themes or the organizational patterns coincide with the reading matter being taught in the other parts of your course. In addition, if sentence writing is of utmost concern, it is possible to work through the sentence part of all the units before working on paragraphs.
3. *Individualize.* Not all students will need to do all the activities. Because of the number of different activities, it is possible to individualize the writing course. For example, in Sentences, after the discourse markers are presented and *Using Discourse Markers* is completed, the students who require practice can work

through the *Guided Writing* activities, while those who are able can proceed immediately to *Write Your Own Sentences*.

Similarly, it is possible to tailor Paragraphs to the needs of a class as a whole as well as to individual students. For instance, *Class Composition* and *Guided Writing* provide three carefully structured writing activities. The class which requires much guidance can work on the class composition as well as on one of the *Guided Writing* topics as a group. On the other hand, students who do not require so much guidance from the teacher could work through the *Class Composition* activity either individually or in pairs or small groups. They could write their paragraphs on transparencies for comparison with the class effort. This technique can lead to good discussion, analysis, and suggestions. In addition, students who do not need so much practice could do either *Class Composition* or *Guided Writing* and then move on to *Write Your Own Paragraph*. Such students might benefit more from writing two "free" paragraphs than from writing one guided and one free paragraph.

In short, make the text work for you: use it as a springboard, a catalyst, an invitation to writing.

CONTENTS

Acknowledgments	iv
To the Teacher	v
Chapter 1 An Introduction	1
Chapter 2 Making/Supporting Generalizations	16
Chapter 3 Enumeration	30
Chapter 4 Comparison I: Talking about Differences	40
Chapter 5 Comparison II: Talking about Similarities	52
Chapter 6 Definition	62
Chapter 7 Cause and Result I: Causes	69
Chapter 8 Cause and Result II: Results	81
Chapter 9 Static Description	91
Chapter 10 Consolidation	98
Teacher's Notes and Answer Key	103

1

AN INTRODUCTION

SENTENCES

Sentences can relate to each other in many different ways. For example, they can show contrast, add information, give examples, or show result. Certain words, called discourse markers, give clues about these relationships. In this text the term *discourse marker* refers to many different parts of speech, all of which act like road signs to tell what lies ahead in the discourse. If you use these markers when you write, the organization of your ideas will be clearer for your reader.

You probably already know some of these markers and the relationships or functions they indicate. In this chapter you will look at some discourse markers which express addition, contrast, and result. In later chapters you will learn about other discourse markers to express these functions as well as others.

Clause relationship	Discourse markers		
	1 Coordinators	2 Subordinators	3 Adverbial connectives
1. Addition (the second clause adds information to the first)	[A] and [B]		[A]; [in addition, B]
2. Contrast (the ideas in the two clauses contrast)	[A] but [B]	(Although A), [B]	[A]; [however, B]
3. Cause/result (the first clause states the cause, the second the result)	[A] so [B]	(Because A), [B]	[A]; [as a result, B]

[ ] = independent clause; ( ) = subordinate clause.
 Note the position of the discourse marker: In column 1 the discourse marker is between the independent clauses. In column 2 the discourse marker is at the beginning of the subordinate clause. In column 3 the discourse marker is within the second independent clause, usually at the beginning.

The chart above has three columns. Each column represents one of the grammatical ways of linking sentences.

Column 1: Coordinators Column 1 contains discourse markers called coordinating conjunctions or coordinators. These words can link or join independent clauses. When independent clauses are linked in this way, each clause is considered of equal importance.

$$\text{[A]} \quad \begin{array}{c} \text{and} \\ \text{but} \\ \text{so} \end{array} \quad \text{[B]}$$

Punctuation: The use of the comma before coordinators varies. A comma is frequently used before *but.* If the independent clauses are short, the comma before the coordinator is often omitted.

Column 2: Subordinators Column 2 contains discourse markers called subordinate conjunctions or subordinators. When a subordinator is used at the beginning of a clause, that clause is made subordinate to or less important grammatically than the other clause, which is then the main clause. The subordinate clause can come before or after the main clause.

$$\text{(Although A), [B]}$$
$$\text{or} \quad \text{[B] (although A)}$$

Punctuation: If the subordinate clause precedes the main clause, a comma follows the subordinate clause. If the main clause is first, the comma is often omitted.

Column 3: Adverbial connectives Column 3 contains discourse markers called adverbial connectives. These words link independent clauses. Adverbial connectives can always be placed at the beginning of the second clause. (Certain markers of this type can be placed within or at the end of the second independent clause. Such placement will be considered in later chapters.)

Punctuation: If the first independent clause ends with a period, the adverbial connective is capitalized.

$$\text{[A]. [However, B]}$$

If the first clause ends in a semicolon, the adverbial connective is not capitalized.

$$\text{[A]; [however, B]}$$

Note: Whatever the punctuation before the adverbial connective, a comma follows it.

Exercise 1 Using Discourse Markers

Coordinators, subordinators, and adverbial connectives serve a double purpose: they link sentences and they also indicate what kind of relationship exists between these sentences.

A. ADDITION Consider these two sentences. The second adds information to the first.

The striking workers want higher wages.   **They want better working conditions.**

You can link these sentences with two kinds of discourse marker.

Coordinator

The striking workers want higher wages *and* they (*also*) want better working conditions.

Note: And is a neutral linking word. To stress the idea that information is added, *also* is often included.

Adverbial connective

The striking workers want higher wages; *in addition*, they want better working conditions.

Now, you link the following sentences. Use the kind of discourse marker for addition indicated and the punctuation required by that kind of discourse marker.

Very small computers are advantageous because they are portable.   **They use only small amounts of power.**

1. *Coordinator* _____

   _____

   _____

2. *Adverbial connective* _____

   _____

   _____

B. CONTRAST   Consider these two sentences which contrast ideas.

I thought I would learn English quickly.   **After six months, I am still not fluent.**

You can link these sentences using a discourse marker from each of the three columns in the chart.

Coordinator

I thought I would learn English quickly *but* after six months I am still not fluent.

Subordinator

***Although* I thought I would learn English quickly, after six months I am still not fluent.**

4 AN INTRODUCTION: Sentences

Adverbial connective

I thought I would learn English quickly. However, after six months I am still not fluent.

These three discourse markers are used to express contrast. They can also be used, as in the preceding examples, to express contrast-concession; that is, they indicate that one idea is surprising or unexpected in relation to the other (i.e., the person is surprised about not being fluent after six months).

Now you link the following sentences which contrast ideas. Use the kind of discourse marker indicated and the punctuation required by each kind of discourse marker.

Cigarettes are unhealthy.   **People continue to smoke.**

1. *Coordinator* _____

   _____

2. *Subordinator* _____

   _____

3. *Adverbial connective* _____

   _____

C. CAUSE/RESULT Consider these two sentences expressing cause and result.

    Cause   *Result*
The exam was very difficult.   **Very few students passed.**

Like the sentences expressing contrast, these sentences can be linked using discourse markers from each of the three columns.

Coordinator

The examination was difficult so very few students passed.

Note: So is a very informal word. It is used to indicate result in speaking and in informal writing.

Subordinator

Because the examination was difficult, very few students passed.

Adverbial connective

The examination was difficult; as a result, very few students passed.

AN INTRODUCTION: Sentences

Now you link the following cause and result sentences. Use the kind of discourse marker indicated and the punctuation required by each kind of discourse marker.

Cause
The lake is polluted.

Result
The fish are dying.

1. *Coordinator* _____

2. *Subordinator* _____

3. *Adverbial connective* _____

Exercise 2 Sentence Combining

Work alone or with a partner. Read the following pairs of sentences and decide if the relationship between them is addition, contrast, or cause/result. Then rewrite the sentence pairs, joining them with an appropriate discourse marker. Remember to use the punctuation required by the kind of discourse marker you have chosen.

1. Overpopulation is becoming an increasingly serious problem. Many families continue to have large numbers of children.

2. The government has limited the number of foreign students entering the country. Universities have raised foreign student tuition fees.

3. The workers' salaries weren't high enough. They decided to go on strike.

4. In the legends of North America the dragon is a threatening animal. In the tales of China, the dragon represents good luck.

6 AN INTRODUCTION: Sentences

5. TV sets have become cheaper to manufacture and sell. More people own sets.

   _____
   _____

6. Some students try to cheat on exams by copying somebody's answers. Others cheat by writing notes on their hands or cuffs.

   _____
   _____

7. Insects do not speak. Certain insects, like bees, can communicate by doing a special dance which shows where nectar is.

   _____
   _____

Exercise 3 Additional Practice

Work alone or with a partner. In each of the following groups of three sentences, there are two relationships. Decide if the relationships are addition, contrast, or result. Use appropriate discourse markers to link the sentences and show the required relationships. Remember to punctuate carefully.

1. The fathers were unemployed. The sons had no hope for their own future. They demonstrated angrily against the government.

   _____
   _____
   _____

2. The space shuttle was ready to return to earth. The weather conditions in the landing zone were poor. The descent was delayed twenty-four hours.

   _____
   _____
   _____

3. A woman is often paid less money than a man for doing the same job. Women are becoming resentful. They are getting militant.

   _____
   _____
   _____

Exercise 4 Write Your Own Sentences

1. Write a sentence of contrast. Use an appropriate discourse marker.

   _____

   _____

2. Write a sentence of cause and result. Use an appropriate discourse marker.

   _____

   _____

3. Write a sentence of addition. Use an appropriate discourse marker.

   _____

   _____

PARAGRAPHS

In this section you will see how sentences relate to each other and work together in paragraphs.

EXPLANATION

What is a paragraph? A paragraph is a group of sentences developing one main idea. Usually this main idea is stated in the first sentence, called the topic sentence. This topic sentence gives the focus the paragraph will have. The rest of the sentences support or develop the main idea. Often the last sentence acts as a conclusion, summarizing, reinforcing, or emphasizing the main idea.

FORMAT

The format of a paragraph looks like this:

> **Topic sentence: This can be a question or statement. Note that the topic sentence is indented on the line. Support: Support for the topic sentence can be in the form of examples, facts, details, statistics, an explanation, a definition, a comparison, a contrast, a cause or causes, a result or results, a combination of these. The support sentences begin on the same line on which the topic sentence ends. Concluding sentence: This is a statement or a question to "drive home" the main point of the paragraph. This sentence follows on the same line as the last support sentence.**

TOPIC SENTENCE

The topic sentence introduces the paragraph. It gives the topic and usually the focus or point of view the paragraph will develop.

Examples
Very small computers have enormous advantages.
Topic: small computers
Focus: advantages

Computers are threatening people's jobs in many industries.
Topic: computers
Focus: job threat

Exercise 1

Read the following topic sentences from the paragraphs you will be working with in the next few pages. For each, fill in the required information. Work alone, or in groups.

1. Many ways of communicating exist that do not utilize language.

   Topic: ways of communicating

   Focus: _____

2. There are three kinds of book owners.

   Topic: _____

   Focus: _____

3a. The Copper Kettle and Pierre's are the latest additions to the restaurant scene in this city; they are similar in several respects.

   Topic: the two restaurants, The Copper Kettle and Pierre's

   Focus: _____

 b. In all other respects these two restaurants differ.

   Topic: the two restaurants, The Copper Kettle and Pierre's

   Focus: _____

4a. Anorexia nervosa is an emotional illness in which the sufferer doesn't let herself eat.

   Topic: _____

 b. What causes anorexia?

   Topic: _____

   Focus: _____

ORGANIZATIONAL PATTERNS

Exercise 2

In Exercise 1 you learned the topic and in some cases the focus of each paragraph. Now read the full paragraphs to see how each is organized. Work either in groups or with your teacher.

1. *Generalization Supported by Examples* The topic sentence is supported by examples of nonverbal communication.

> Many ways of communicating exist that do not utilize language. Cries of warning and aggression, of contentment and affection, are forms of communication not limited to men. Or, on the human level, the dirty look, which may convey worlds of meaning, does not involve language. Gestures, too, are forms of communication, although these seem always involved with culturally defined habits. The nod of the head means "yes" to the American, but a single nod in the Middle East is a clear "no." Plainly, there are many ways of conveying messages, of which language is but the major one for human beings.[1]

What examples of communication without the use of language are given in this paragraph?

2. *Enumeration* The topic sentence is developed with information about three kinds of book owners.

> There are three kinds of book owners. The first has all the standard sets and best-sellers—unread, untouched. (This deluded individual owns wood pulp and ink, not books.) The second has a great many books—a few of them read through, most of them dipped into, but all of them as clean and shiny as the day they were bought. (This person would probably like to make books his own, but is restrained by a false respect for their physical appearance.) The third has a few books or many—every one of them dog-eared and dilapidated, shaken and loosened by continual use, marked and scribbled in from front to back. (This man owns books.)[2]

Describe each kind of book owner.

---

1. Reprinted with permission of McGraw-Hill from *Anthropology: The Study of Man*, by E. A. Hoebel, 1966, p. 33.
2. Reprinted with permission of McGraw-Hill from *Study Skills for Students of English as a Second Language*, by R. C. Yorkey, 1970.

3a. *Comparison/Similarities* The paragraph supports the topic sentence by showing similarities between the two restaurants.

> The Copper Kettle and Pierre's are the latest additions to the restaurant scene in this city; they are similar in several respects. Both are located in the trendy market area, both have the required number of hanging plants, and both serve the now fashionable quiches, spinach salad, and carrot cake.

What features are the same in both restaurants?

b. *Comparison/Differences* The paragraph supports the topic sentence by showing the differences between the two restaurants.

> In all other respects these two restaurants differ. The Copper Kettle caters to a younger crowd. That means moderate prices, many variations of hamburger, and a background of pop music. Pierre's, on the other hand, is attracting a different group altogether. The prices are higher; the food tends toward the gourmet and the music to the classical. I found both restaurants very enjoyable; they're worth trying.

In what ways are The Copper Kettle and Pierre's different?

4a. *Description* The topic sentence defines anorexia nervosa. The paragraph describes who is affected by the disease.

> Anorexia nervosa is an emotional illness in which the sufferer doesn't let herself eat. The anorexic, in fact, starves herself. This condition affects girls between the ages of 12 and 18. (Only one in fifteen anorexics is male.) The typical victim is a bright, sensitive person from an upper-middle-class or wealthy family. She has high expectations of herself and is self-critical even when her performance is excellent. She is often close with her parents. The anorexic's parents are conscious of weight or appearance and are concerned about athletics or fatness. They may have high expectations for achievement from their children. Sometimes they are overprotective of or overinvolved with their children.

Describe who suffers from this disease, what kind of personality the victim has, and what kind of family and family relationships the victim has.

b. *Cause/Result* The paragraph supports the topic sentence by giving causes for the result, anorexia nervosa.

> What causes anorexia? There are many causes. For some anorexics, the denial of food leads to a pleasurable sense of self-control. By controlling how much she eats, she is controlling her body and feels she has somehow gained

control of her life. Another cause is fear of growing up. Severe weight loss can bring about physical changes (like loss of menstruation), allowing temporary avoidance of the stresses of adolescence. Family conflicts can also contribute to anorexia.

What are three possible causes of this illness?

CONCLUDING SENTENCES

Single paragraphs are most effective if there is a final sentence which reinforces the main idea of the paragraph. Not all paragraphs that you read will have such a concluding sentence, however. The reason for this is that in longer discourse one paragraph leads to another and the conclusion is stated in the last paragraph.

There are different ways to conclude a paragraph. One way is to restate the topic sentence. However, don't use the exact words. Reformulate the topic sentence, or, if it is appropriate, restate the topic sentence as a question.

Topic Sentence
English is hard for me to learn.

Concluding Sentence
Reformulation: I hope I can overcome these difficulties.

Question: Can you see now why English is so difficult for me to learn?

Another way to conclude a paragraph is to summarize, in one sentence, the contents of the paragraph. Adverbial connectives such as *in short, to sum up, for these reasons* are useful for introducing such summarizing statements.

Topic Sentence
Can we learn anything from television?

Concluding Sentence
In short, TV has much to teach us if we choose our programs carefully.

When it is appropriate, the final sentence of a paragraph can also be a recommendation, a suggestion, or a warning.

Exercise 3

Reread the sample paragraphs in Exercise 2. Some of the paragraphs have concluding sentences and some don't. Which of the paragraphs have concluding sentences? Where there *is* a concluding sentence, decide if it is a restatement of the topic sentence, a summary of the paragraph, or a recommendation.

12 AN INTRODUCTION: Paragraphs

Exercise 4

Below are groups of sentences which could form the body of a paragraph. However, they require a topic sentence and concluding sentence. Work in pairs or groups. Read the sentence groups carefully to discover the main idea. Then, in the space provided write the topic and concluding sentences.

1. Choose topic sentence *a, b,* or *c* below and explain your choice.

   (Topic sentence) _____

   _____

   For example, geography is needed for an understanding of economics because natural resources and transportation affect production and distribution of goods. Changes in engineering affect economics. Psychology is also related because it can help the economist understand why some people want some products and not others. Because it is necessary to calculate averages and trends, mathematics is important to economics. Finally, the language and the writing method used may help or hinder trade.

   (Concluding sentence) _____

   _____

   Topic sentence:
   a. Economics is an important field of study.
   b. Economics is related to many other fields of study.
   c. Economics is tied to geography and psychology.

2. (Topic sentence) _____

   _____

   The popular pocket calculator is an example of a tiny computer for everyday use—shopping, banking, or any activity requiring numerical calculations. A similar device, using the alphabet instead of numbers, can be used for simple translations. In a doctor's office, computers can take medical records. Some experiments are even being done with computers making diagnoses of common complaints. Computers can make legal matters easier by quickly recalling relevant precedents. Many areas of teaching, such as languages and mathematics, can utilize computers too. (Concluding sentence) ____

   _____

   _____

3. (Topic sentence) _____

   _____

   Everyone knows about the presence of caffeine in coffee and tea, but it may not be generally known that caffeine is present in cola drinks. Products made with cocoa, like hot chocolate and chocolate bars, include this stimulant too, although its presence is not readily evident to us. Prescription and nonprescription drugs used for headaches and

AN INTRODUCTION: Paragraphs   13

migraines are another hidden source of caffeine. (Concluding sentence) _____

_____

_____

4.   (Topic sentence) _____

_____

Public places like restaurants and shopping centers are filled with cigarette smoke. Viruses from cold and flu victims are in every office and store. Exhaust fumes from cars, buses, and trucks fill the streets with carbon monoxide. Even the parks carry poisons and pollens that plague hay fever sufferers. (Concluding sentence) _____

_____

_____

AUDIENCE, PURPOSE, AND CONTENT

Whenever you write, you write for a specific audience and you have a specific purpose. The audience and purpose influence the language you use and the content of what you write. For example, if you are writing your friend to invite him to visit you, the letter will be quite different from a letter in which you ask him for advice about some of your problems. Both of these letters would be very different from a letter to the registrar of a university asking about admission requirements.

In the following chapters you will consider your audience and purpose whenever you write paragraphs.

Exercise 5 Audience

Read the note and memo which follow.

Dear Mom,
    I'm broke! Can you lend me $5.00?
        Your ever-loving son,
            John ☺

14 AN INTRODUCTION: Paragraphs

Memo to the Dean

Re: Supplies Budget

At the present time, the supplies budget is over-extended by $3000.00. There are several reasons for this:

1. The budget was too small to begin with.
2. There have been unexpected repair expenses for lab equipment.
3. Inflation has increased faster than our budget.

Are any funds available at this time to help cover this deficit?
B. Smith
Department Chairman

Discuss in groups or with your class.
1. The purpose of the note and the memo is the same. What does each writer want?
2. The note and memo have different audiences: Who is the note for? Who is the memo for?
3. The difference in audience affects the form and content of the note and memo. In what ways do the note and memo differ? (Consider length, words used to explain the situation and make the request, the use of first person, the presence/absence of explanations.)
4. If you were writing for experts (people who know a great deal about your discipline) or laymen (ordinary people), there would be differences in both language and content. (*a*) For which group could you use specific terminology? (*b*) For which group would you use everyday language and, perhaps, definitions. (*c*) For which group could you go more deeply into the subject?

Exercise 6 *Purpose*

1. Think about the writing you have done in the past week. What were the purposes of your writing (e.g., a letter describing what you were doing, a request for information, a reminder)? List these purposes on the board.
2. In English certain words are very useful for expressing particular purposes. Below is a list of some purposes for writing and some vocabulary appropriate to each purpose. Read the list; then add purposes and vocabulary of your own.

Purpose	Vocabulary
Advise	Should; it's a good idea; advise
Warn	Must; have to, imperative of verbs
Express opinion	In my opinion; I think; I believe
Report/inform	(No opinions; objective fact)
Recommend	I believe, think
Compare/contrast	Same; different; better; worse

Exercise 7 Content

Read the following information.

Effects of Smoking

Short-Term Effects:
   For the novice:
      Increase in heart rate and blood pressure
      Drop in skin temperature
      Faster breathing
      Possible diarrhea and vomiting
      Stimulation of central nervous system
   For the habitual smoker:
      Tolerance to the preceding effects develops

Long-Term Effects:
   General health:
      Probable association with cancer of the lung, mouth, and respiratory tract
      Relationship with respiratory diseases—e.g., emphysema, bronchitis
      Higher probability of development of coronary heart disease
      Greater likelihood of occurrence of stomach ulcers
   Women:
      Tendency toward earlier menopause
      Tendency toward heart disease if oral contraceptives are also used
      Pregnancy:
         Smaller babies
         More premature babies, stillborns, and miscarriages

Since your audience and purpose affect the content of what you write, discuss in groups or with your class which of the facts in the chart you would choose if you were a journalist writing an article about the results of recent experiments on the effects of smoking, a public health nurse giving a lecture to expectant mothers, or a health teacher preparing a lesson for teenagers.

Now that you have considered paragraphs in general, you are ready to proceed.

2
MAKING/SUPPORTING GENERALIZATIONS

In this chapter you will learn about generalizing. A generalization is a broad statement. It is true or applicable in most cases, sometimes in all. You generalize when you consider evidence and then draw a conclusion from it.

For example, a student from another country wants to know if there is a lot of rain in your country. Five years ago and again last year, it was dry, but in all other years, the pattern has been long rainy periods. You can therefore make this generalization:

> ***On the whole***, there is a lot of rain in my country.
> or There is *usually* a lot of rain in my country.

In this chapter you will learn how to write generalizations and how to support them.

SENTENCES

There are different levels of generality; that is, some generalizations apply all the time; some apply only in some cases. In the following chart, consider the percentages on the left in relation to the discourse markers for generalizing (see Teachers' Notes).

Discourse Markers for Generalizing

	Group A	Group B	
	Adverbial connectives	Determiners	Adverbs
100%		All No, none Every	Always Never
	In general Generally (speaking) On the whole	Most	Usually
		Many	Often
		Some	Sometimes
0%			

You can use discourse markers from different columns to make generalizations having the same degree of generality. For example, you can say:

> ***Generally***, the students at my college are friendly to newcomers.
> or ***Most*** students at my college are friendly to newcomers.
> or The students at my college are ***usually*** friendly to newcomers.

MAKING GENERALIZATIONS AND PROVIDING STATISTICAL SUPPORT

Exercise 1A Analyzing a Survey: Making Generalizations

A professor of a graduate class asked his students if they preferred their final grade in the course based on an examination or on his evaluation of their work throughout the year. These are the results of his survey:

Student	Grade in course so far	Prefer exam	Prefer evaluation
1	A	×	
2	A		×
3	A	×	
4	A	×	
5	B	×	
6	B	×	
7	B	×	
8	B		×
9	C	×	
10	C		×
11	C		×
12	C		×
13	C	×	
14	D	×	
15	D	×	
16	F	×	
17	F	×	

Analyze the survey and make generalizations.

1a. How many students are in the class? _____

b. How many want an exam? _____

c. How many want an evaluation? _____

d. Now write a generalization about the students' preference for an exam or an evaluation. Use the kind of discourse marker for generalizing indicated.

Connective _____.

Determiner _____.

2a. How many A and B students are there? _____

b. How many want an exam? _____

c. How many want an evaluation? _____

18 MAKING/SUPPORTING GENERALIZATIONS: Sentences

d. Write a generalization about the A and B students' preference for an exam or an evaluation. Use the kind of discourse marker for generalizing indicated.

Connective _____.

Determiner _____.

3*a.* How many C students are there? _____

b. How many want an exam? _____

c. How many want an evaluation? _____

d. Write a generalization about the C students' preference for an exam or evaluation. Use the appropriate marker from the determiner group.

Determiner _____.

4*a.* How many D and F students are there? _____

b. How many want an exam? _____

c. How many want an evaluation? _____

d. Write a generalization about the D and F students' preference for an exam or an evaluation. Use the appropriate marker from the determiner group.

Determiner _____.

Exercise 1B Analyzing a Survey: Supporting Generalizations by Statistics

We can support or prove generalizations in several ways: by statistics, examples, or specific detail. In this exercise we will practice using statistics to prove generalizations.

Generalization	*Support by Statistics*
In Professor Page's class, many students preferred a final exam.	Twelve chose the exam and five asked for an evaluation. In other words, 70% preferred the exam to the evaluation.

Consider the C, D, and F students in Professor Page's class.
1. Write a generalization about their preference for an exam or an evaluation. Use an appropriate discourse marker for generalizing.
2. Support your generalization with statistics drawn from the survey.

Exercise 2 Making Your Own Survey

In this exercise you will make your own survey of students' preference for an examination or an evaluation. Also include other information that might be of interest (e.g., country of origin, sex, age, graduate or undergraduate level). Your chart should look like this:

Student	Preference		Sex		Level		Age	Country
	Exam	Evaluation	Male	Female	Grad.	Undergrad.		
1								
2								
3								
4								
5								
6								
7								
8								
9								
10								
11								
12								

Work in groups: Group 1 survey your ESL class. Group 2 survey another (ESL) class. Group 3 survey a random group of students (in the cafeteria or in the library).

Note: Make sure your sample is large enough.

When you approach your "subjects," explain that you are a student doing a survey for your English class. Ask them if they will help you.

Exercise 3 *Analyzing Your Survey*

Work with your group to analyze the data you gathered in your survey. Consider questions such as these: What was the overall preference of the people you surveyed—an examination or an evaluation? Which did most men/women prefer? Which did most graduates/undergraduates prefer?

Exercise 4 *Write Your Own Sentences: Generalizations Supported by Statistics*

Work with your group. Based on your answers in Exercise 3, write generalizations. Remember to use appropriate discourse markers for generalizing. Then support your generalizations with statistics from your survey (Exercise 2).

1. _____

2. _____

3. _____

4. _____

20 MAKING/SUPPORTING GENERALIZATIONS: Sentences

5. _____
   _____

6. _____
   _____

7. _____
   _____

8. _____
   _____

MAKING GENERALIZATIONS AND PROVIDING SUPPORT BY EXAMPLES

Discourse Markers for Giving Examples: Group A

Adverbial connectives
For instance
For example

Exercise 5 Using Group A Discourse Markers

Examples are often used to prove generalizations. (Sometimes statistics provide the example.)

Generalization	*Example*
Many students have negative reactions to exams.	Some can't sleep or eat.

Many students have negative reactions to exams; *for instance*, some can't sleep or eat.

Generalization	*Example*
Many students have negative reactions to exams.	A recent study revealed that 25% of the students surveyed suffered from insomnia, 15% from stomach problems, and 10% from miscellaneous nervous reactions.

Many students have negative reactions to exams. For instance, a recent study revealed that 25% of the students surveyed suffered from insomnia, 15% from stomach problems, and 10% from miscellaneous nervous reactions.

MAKING/SUPPORTING GENERALIZATIONS: Sentences   21

Join the following sentences, using discourse markers from Group A.

1. *Generalization*   *Example*
    Japan is a land of contrasts.   Graceful old temples stand next to modern buildings of concrete and steel.

    _____

    _____

2. *Generalization*   *Example*
    Australia and England have some similarities.   In both countries tea is a favorite drink, cricket is a popular sport, and driving is on the left.

    _____

    _____

3. *Generalization*   *Example*
    Most clerical jobs are held by women.   In this country, women do 80% of the clerical work.

    _____

    _____

Discourse Markers for Giving Examples: Group B

Prepositions	Noun
Such as (+ noun) Like (+ noun)	(An) example (is) . . .

Exercise 6   *Using Group B Discourse Markers*

            Generalization   *Examples*
Immunization has stopped the spread   Polio, smallpox
of many diseases.

Preposition
Immunization has stopped the spread of many diseases *such as* polio and smallpox.

Noun
Immunization has stopped the spread of many diseases. Two *examples* are polio and smallpox.

22 MAKING/SUPPORTING GENERALIZATIONS: Sentences

Write sentences about the information below. Use the kind of discourse marker indicated to introduce the example.

1. *Generalization*
    Computers have entered many areas of our lives.

    Examples
    Airlines, banks, hospitals, supermarkets, and ticket offices

    a. Preposition: _____

    b. Noun: _____

2. *Generalization*
    There are many home remedies for the common cold.

    Example
    Hot milk or tea mixed with honey and whiskey

    a. Preposition: _____

    b. Noun: _____

3. *Generalization*
    English language students have difficulty with the spelling and pronunciation of certain words.

    Examples
    Through, cough, bough

    a. Preposition: _____

    b. Noun: _____

Exercise 7 Write Your Own Sentences: Generalizations Supported by Examples

Write generalizations about your impressions of the country or city you are now living in (the people, weather, food, traffic, lifestyle, entertainment, role of men/women, etc.). Use the discourse markers for generalizing indicated. Then support each generalization with an example. Use an appropriate discourse marker to introduce your example.

Example There are *usually* cultural differences in patterns of communication. *For example*, the people from different cultures vary in how fast or loudly they talk as well as how close they stand to the person they are talking to.

MAKING/SUPPORTING GENERALIZATIONS: Sentences   23

1. Generally speaking, _____
   _____
   _____

2. On the whole, _____
   _____
   _____

3. All _____
   _____
   _____

4. Everyone _____
   _____
   _____

5. Most _____
   _____
   _____

6. Some _____
   _____
   _____

7. _____ (never) _____
   _____
   _____

8. _____ (always) _____
   _____
   _____

9. _____ (usually) _____
   _____
   _____

PARAGRAPHS

Exercise 1   Read and Analyze

Read the paragraphs below.

A. SUPPORT BY STATISTICS

On the whole, the percentage of women in many areas of the business world is increasing. In 1971, 4% of the graduates with masters of business administration degrees in the United States were women; by 1980, women graduates had risen to 19%. *Furthermore*, women in management more than doubled their numbers between 1970 and 1978. The latest data show that they make up nearly 40% of the work force in companies of 100 or more employees. *As well*, they hold 17% of all managerial and supervisory jobs. Although progress has been slow, the doors to the business world are finally opening for women.

1. According to the topic sentence, what is the topic of this paragraph?
2. The topic is developed by the addition of specific facts about the numbers or percentages of women in different areas of the business world. Fill in the outline below with facts from the paragraph.

Year	Number or percent of women	Area of business world
1971	_____	Masters of business administration
1980	_____	_____
____	_____	_____
	_____	_____
	_____	_____

3. Note the italicized words; these are two new discourse markers for adding information.
4. Which discourse marker introduces the generalization?
5. What part of the concluding sentence refers to the topic sentence?
6. Is the purpose of the paragraph to request information, give information, or make a suggestion?

MAKING/SUPPORTING GENERALIZATIONS: Paragraphs

Look at the following discourse markers for adding information.

Discourse Markers for Addition: Group A
Adverbial Connectives

In addition As well Also	Add information
Furthermore Moreover	Add information and expand meaning
In fact Indeed	Add information and reinforce what was said

B. SUPPORT BY EXAMPLES

Generally speaking, English is a difficult language for me to learn. For example, vocabulary is a problem. Sometimes several words like "thin," "slender," "skinny," or "slim" have almost the same meaning. How can you tell which word to use? Pronunciation is hard also. My tongue will not make sounds such as "th," "g," and "k." Furthermore, writing presents a whole group of different obstacles: grammar, word order, and spelling. These are only some of the difficulties I have with this language.

1. What is the topic of the paragraph according to the topic sentence?
2. The topic is developed by the addition of examples. Fill in the outline below with information from the paragraph.

Problem	*Example and/or Explanation*
Vocabulary	Examples _____
	Explanation of difficulty _____
	_____
_____	Examples _____
_____	Examples _____

3. Find the discourse markers used for generalizing, adding information, and giving examples.
4. Instead of repeating "difficult" and "problem," the writer used synonyms. Find the synonyms he used.
5. Is the purpose of the paragraph to express an opinion and explain it, advise and explain advice, or suggest and explain the suggestion?

MAKING/SUPPORTING GENERALIZATIONS: Paragraphs

**Format for Paragraphs of Generalization
Supported by Addition of Specific Detail**

Topic sentence: **A generalization or general statement**
Support   ⎰ Statistics
   (discourse markers ⎱ Examples
   for addition)   ⎱ Facts
Concluding sentence

Note: In your own writing, don't introduce every fact with a discourse marker. Use discourse markers judiciously!

Exercise 2   Class Composition

Do this exercise with your teacher and class, using the blackboard to build your paragraph together.

1. What aspects of English are most difficult for you? Write these on the board. Then write specific examples of each kind of difficulty. E.g., difficulty—spelling; examples—threw, through
2. Now write a paragraph to explain why learning English is difficult. Your audience is other students.
   Topic Sentence: Write a topic sentence similar to the one in Exercise 1: "Generally speaking, English is a difficult language for me to learn."
   Support: Support your topic sentence by referring to the major difficulties and examples from question 1, above. Use appropriate discourse markers to introduce examples and add information.
   Concluding Sentence: Reformulate your topic sentence, or summarize the information in your support.

Exercise 3   Guided Writing

Do either A or B.

A. You are an economic analyst, writing a report to inform the general public about trends in mortgage rates. Consider the information in the following chart.

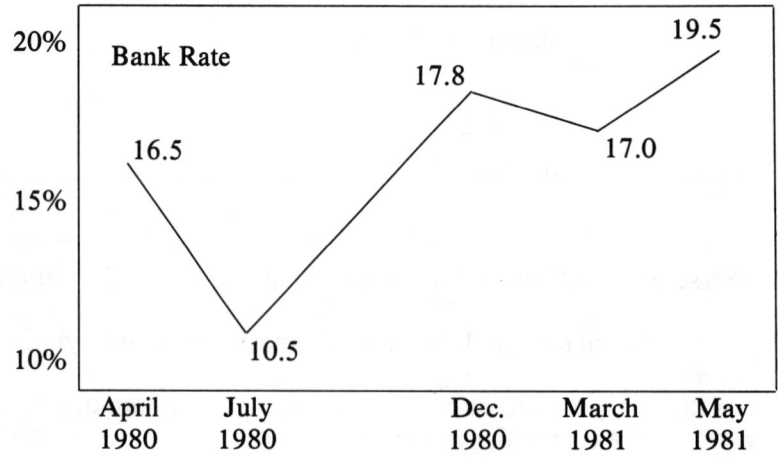

1. *Topic Sentence:* (a) What was the bank rate in each month referred to? (b) Has the trend, on the whole, been up or down? (c) The topic sentence for your paragraph should be a generalization based on your answers to (a) and (b) above. Use an appropriate discourse marker for generalizing.
2. *Support:* Use the statistics from the chart to support your generalization. Use appropriate discourse markers for giving examples and adding information.
3. *Concluding Sentence:* Considering the trend, predict what future interest rates might be. (*Optional:* If your purpose were to advise the general public about investments and loans, given the trend in bank rates, what advice would you give someone who wants to borrow money from the bank, or someone who wants to invest money in a bank certificate and earn interest? This advice could form your concluding sentence.)

B. Write a review for your classmates of a restaurant in this city.
1. *Topic Sentence:* Make a general statement about the restaurant: is it excellent, good, fair, or bad?
2. *Support:* Support your topic sentence with specific information and examples of the food, prices, service, and atmosphere. Use appropriate discourse markers for giving examples and adding information.
3. *Concluding Sentence:* If the restaurant is good, recommend it to your classmates; if it isn't good, state that you do not recommend it.

Exercise 4 Write Your Own Paragraph

A topic must be narrow enough to develop in a single paragraph. You have to break a broad topic down into subdivisions so that you can deal with that section within the limits of one paragraph.

For example, consider how the following broad topics are broken down into several mini-topics. Some of these can be subdivided into even smaller topics.

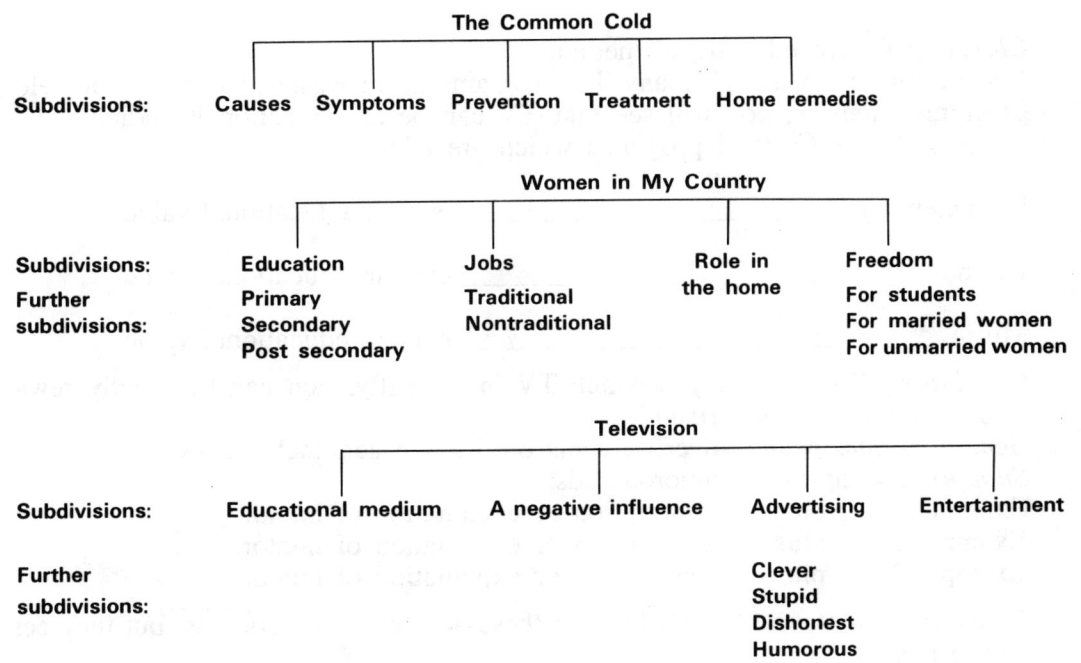

28   MAKING/SUPPORTING GENERALIZATIONS: Paragraphs

A. With your teacher, select a topic from the following list and break it down into smaller topics or subdivisions.

<table>
<tr><td>Smoking</td><td>Money</td></tr>
<tr><td>Adjusting to North American society</td><td>Aging</td></tr>
<tr><td>Freedom</td><td>Entertainment in this city</td></tr>
<tr><td>Fashions</td><td>Restaurants in this city</td></tr>
<tr><td>Drugs</td><td>Energy</td></tr>
<tr><td>Pollution</td><td>Ecology</td></tr>
<tr><td>Advertising</td><td>Space</td></tr>
<tr><td>Computers</td><td>Medicine</td></tr>
<tr><td>Video games</td><td></td></tr>
</table>

Once you have subdivided your topic, evaluate each section. Ask yourself: Do I have something to say about this topic? Do I have, or can I find, details to support my view? If the answer is yes, formulate a generalization for your topic sentence. Then support your topic sentence by listing specific details—examples, facts, statistics. If the answer to the question is no, choose another section of the topic and repeat the process until you *can* answer yes.

Example:

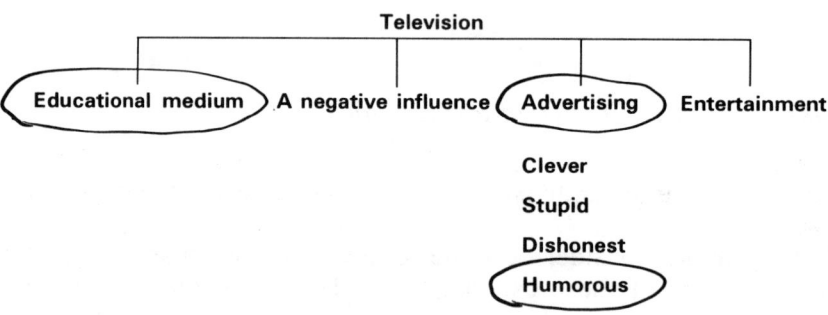

1. *Choice:* TV—An educational medium
   Generalization: Although many TV programs are a waste of time, if you select TV programs carefully, you will see that TV can be an educational medium.
   Support: Name kinds of programs which are educational.

   Documentary _____ explain educational value

   Drama _____ explain educational value

   Music _____ explain educational value

   Concluding Sentence: If you watch TV intelligently, you can be greatly rewarded.

2. *Choice:* Humorous advertising
   Generalization: Many advertisements on TV are genuinely funny.
   Support: Examples of humorous ads:
   Example 1   plus   description or explanation of humor.
   Example 2   plus   description or explanation of humor.
   Example 3   plus   description or explanation of humor.

   Concluding Sentence: I don't know if these ads sell their products, but they certainly amuse me.

B. Work in pairs or groups of three.
1. Select a broad topic from the list in A, and subdivide it.
2. Choose one of the subdivisions.
3. Decide on your audience and purpose (your classmates? to express your opinion or to inform?).
4. Make a generalization.
5. Consider what support would be most convincing—examples? statistics? facts? all three? List the specific support you would use. Decide what explanation or elaboration you would need.
6. Write a concluding sentence.
    Note: You don't have to write a paragraph yet. In this exercise, you are working on the plan.

C. Work alone and write your own paragraph. Follow the same procedure as you did in Exercise 2, but use a different topic. Your audience is your class. Your purpose is to inform or to express your opinion.

Remember to use appropriate discourse markers for generalizing, giving examples, and adding information.

EXAM-TYPE QUESTIONS

Paragraphs developed by generalization and support are a useful format to use in answering certain types of exam questions. Often you are asked to discuss or prove a statement.

> "Computers have changed our society." Prove this statement with reference to . . .

This statement becomes the topic sentence of your answer.

> On the whole, computers have changed society.

You then support the topic sentence by drawing on relevant facts, statistics, and/or examples from the material you have been reading or studying. Link these sentences with appropriate discourse markers for examples and/or adding information. Conclude by summarizing the content of the paragraph or rewriting the topic sentence.

Your teacher will give you practice with this type of question relating to your reading or your field of study (see Teachers' Notes).

3

ENUMERATION

Enumeration is useful when you want to list or state a number of factors: reasons, purposes, causes, results, symptoms, advantages, disadvantages, recommendations, changes, etc. When you want to convince, prove, or report, it is very helpful to be able to present such a list of factors. In this chapter you will learn how to write sentences and then paragraphs of enumeration.

SENTENCES

Exercise 1

1. From the topics below, select the one which is most interesting to your class. Then list on the board the advantages, characteristics, reasons, dangers, or benefits as required.

   a. Advantages of learning English.
   b. Characteristics of a successful (language) student.
   c. Characteristics of a good teacher.
   d. Reasons for using robots in industry.
   e. The dangers/benefits of research into cloning.
   f. Necessary changes (or improvements) to _____ .
   g. (Your choice).

2. If you had chosen *b*, you might have written this on your board:

   Characteristics of a successful student: Motivation
   Self-discipline
   Organization

   To make this information into linked sentences we first write a statement which introduces the enumeration.

   A successful student has $\begin{Bmatrix} \text{several} \\ \text{three main} \end{Bmatrix}$ characteristics.

   or   There are $\begin{Bmatrix} \text{several} \\ \text{three main} \end{Bmatrix}$ characteristics which a successful student has.

3. With your class, compose a statement which introduces your enumeration from question 1.

Now consider these discourse markers.

Discourse Markers for Enumerating: Group A

Adverbial connectives

First
Second
Third
Last
Finally

We can write sentences of enumeration using adverbial connectives.

Successful students have several characteristics. *First*, they have motivation. *Second*, they have self-discipline. *Last*, they are organized.

4. Return to number 1 above. Select the three main reasons, advantages, etc., which you listed. Be sure they are in sentence form. Then complete the enumeration you began in number 3 by joining your reasons, advantages, etc., to your introductory statement. Use appropriate adverbial connectives from the chart above to introduce each sentence in your list.

Exercise 2 Using Group A Discourse Markers

Use adverbial connectives to join the following sentences.

1. According to some, our survival on this planet is severely threatened.

    There is growing pollution.
    Population is increasing.
    The nuclear arms race continues to escalate.

    _____

    _____

2. Teenage crime in this city can be reduced in two ways.

    Increase the number of police officers on duty.
    Involve teenagers in meaningful activities.

    _____

3. There are several arguments for using industrial robots.

    They have high productivity.
    They are reliable.
    They can do jobs dangerous or unhealthy for people.

    _____

    _____

ENUMERATION: Sentences

Discourse Markers for Enumerating: Group B

Determiners		Pronouns	
The first (reason)	One ( )	The first (is)	One (is)
The second ( )	Another ( )	The second (is)	Another (is)
The third ( )	A third ( )	The third (is)	A third (is)
The {last/final} ( )		The last (is)	

The sentences of enumeration for Exercise 1 can be rewritten using discourse markers from Group B.

Pronoun
A successful student has several characteristics. *The first* is motivation; *the second* is self-discipline; *the third* is organization.

Determiner/Pronoun
A successful student has several characteristics. *One* characteristic is motivation; *another* is self-discipline; *the last* is organization.

Look at your work from Exercise 1. Experiment with discourse markers from Group B for writing sentences of enumeration.

Exercise 3 Using Group B Discourse Markers

Use the kind of Group B discourse marker indicated to write sentences of enumeration.

1. Nuclear reactions can occur by two different processes.

   Nuclear fission
   Nuclear fusion

   Pronouns _____

   _____

2. According to one professor, there have been two changes in psychology in the past 15 years.

   A movement from a behavioristic to a cognitive approach

   An increased interaction between psychology and other sciences which study people

   Determiner/Pronoun _____

   _____

   _____

   _____

3. The teachers went on strike for three reasons.   Higher wages
　　　　　　　　　　　　　　　　　　　　　　　　More preparation time
　　　　　　　　　　　　　　　　　　　　　　　　Better working conditions

Determiner/Pronoun _____

_____

_____

_____

Exercise 4 Sentence Completion

Work alone or in pairs. Complete the following sentences using appropriate discourse markers for enumerating.

1. There were two main reasons for the students' protest. _____

_____

_____

_____

2. In this country, women have traditionally worked at certain jobs. _____

_____

3. In my opinion there are (two) main explanations for failure among first-year university students. _____

_____

_____

4. (*Name of disease*) has several symptoms. _____

_____

_____

5. I have two recommendations for the prevention of cheating during examinations. _____

_____

_____

34 ENUMERATION: Paragraphs

Exercise 5 Write Your Own Sentences

On a separate piece of paper, write sentences of enumeration on a topic of your choice.

PARAGRAPHS

Exercise 1 Read and Analyze

1. Read the letter below.

Date: January 15, 1982

Inside address:
Mr. B. M. Smith,
Manager,
Fairtown Tools, Inc.
349 Queen Street,
Fairtown, U.S.A.

Salutation: Dear Mr. Smith,

Body of letter (note margins):

   As union representative, I am writing to inform you of the main demands presented by the employees at the strike meeting today. The first is higher wages. The cost of living has increased by 10% but the management of this factory has offered us only a 5% increase. The second demand is improved benefits, such as a dental plan, higher vacation pay, and a more extensive pension plan. The third consideration is the provision of better facilities within the factory. A cafeteria or larger area is vital so that employees can escape the noise of the factory machines at least during lunch. Finally, changes in the work schedule are necessary. For example, staggered hours, shorter shifts, or longer breaks must be considered. These are our demands; we sincerely hope you can meet them before the strike deadline.

Closing:

Sincerely,

John Adam

John Adam
Union Representative,
Local 392

ENUMERATION: Paragraphs   35

2. Fill in the following outline based on the information in the letter.

   Topic (as stated in topic sentence): _____

Demands	Support for each demand
_____	Statistics: _____
_____	Examples: _____
_____	Explanation: _____
_____	Examples: _____

   Concluding sentence: Which words refer to the topic sentence? _____

3. Underline the discourse markers which indicate enumeration.
4. Find and underline one discourse marker which indicates contrast and two which introduce examples.
5. For what audience was this letter written?
6. What is the purpose of the letter?

Format for Paragraphs of Enumeration

Topic sentence: a statement or question which introduces the enumeration. (There are several factors which . . .)

Support:

(discourse marker for enumerating)	Factor 1	plus examples or explanations
(discourse marker for enumerating)	Factor 2	plus examples or explanations
(discourse marker for enumerating)	Factor 3	plus examples or explanations

Concluding sentence: { a summarizing statement / a reformulation / a recommendation / etc. } as required

36 ENUMERATION: Paragraphs

Note: The discourse markers for enumerating on pages 31 and 32 give an objective listing. If you want to indicate your opinion about the importance or significance of a factor, introduce this factor with the markers

> The most important
> The most significant } (reason, cause, etc.)

Exercise 2 Class Composition

Do this exercise with your teacher and class, using the board to build your paragraph together.

1. Read the following letter to the editor which appeared in a national newspaper.

Dear Sir,

I am writing this letter to the newspaper because I want an answer from the people of this city: Why didn't you help me?

On June 23, in the middle of the afternoon I got off the bus at Main and First, and began to walk down First Avenue. Two men approached me. One pushed me down and started to hit me. The other grabbed my wallet. They beat me, severely, and ran.

No one came to help! I know people had seen what had happened: some had gotten off the bus with me; some were shopping; others were going into office buildings. It was the middle of the afternoon and the street was not deserted. As I lay on the sidewalk, bleeding, unable to move, I could not believe this was actually happening—not to me! Not in this lovely city of ours.

I must have passed out then. When I woke up, I was in the hospital. Someone had indeed finally called an ambulance. To that man I have already expressed my gratitude. To those people who saw but would not get involved, I direct my question: Why wouldn't you help me?

Timothy Blackburn

---

2. Discuss with your class and your teacher why people are reluctant to get involved in incidents like the one described in this letter.
3. List the reasons on the board. After each reason, add any explanations or examples necessary to clarify or develop that reason.
4. Now with your class write a letter to the editor in which you give the reasons which explain why people do not get involved in incidents like this one.
   Topic Sentence: Use a topic sentence such as the following: "In my opinion there are _____ reasons which explain why people don't get involved."
   Support: Select from question 3 above the three or four reasons (with explanations and/or examples) which you consider the most significant as explanations of noninvolvement. Use discourse markers for enumerating to introduce each reason.
   Concluding Sentence: Reformulate the topic sentence or summarize the content of your letter.

Exercise 3 Guided Writing

Do either A or B. Use the format for enumerating.

A. You are a student at a language school. The students have had a meeting to discuss the problems they are experiencing at the school. Now, as the student representative, you have to write a letter to Mr. Robertson, the director, enumerating the problems and asking for a solution.

Read the following minutes of the students' meeting. Use the information there as the basis of your letter to Mr. Robertson. (Note the conventions of letter writing in the letter in Exercise 1.)

```
Minutes - Student meeting - Sept. 10
- meeting began - 3:30
- representatives from all classes present
- the problems were discussed
    1) classes are too large - 22, 20, 26, 21, etc.
        - maximum should be 12
    2) books are too expensive - most
        students work or are on scholarships
        Can't afford $25 per book
    3) lab is inadequate
        - too small
        - too few tape recorders
        - often the tape recorders don't work
    4) we don't speak enough
        - classes are too big
        - too much time in class is
            for reading and writing

- decision - write letter to director; list
    problems; ask for solutions.
- next meeting - Sept. 17
- purpose - report on letter to director.
```

Topic Sentence: In the first two sentences tell why you are writing and make a statement which introduces your enumeration of the problems.
Support: List and explain the problems based on the minutes of the students' meeting. Use discourse markers for enumerating to introduce each problem.
Concluding Sentence: Ask the director to consider solutions to the problems.

B. The university publishes an orientation pamphlet for new students. You work for the Health Service which wants you to write a paragraph for the pamphlet on ways students can handle stress.

The Health Service has given you the following information from a mental health association.

Tips for Relieving Pressure of Everyday Living

Talk—Talking brings relief and gives perspective.
Escape—Go to a movie, read a book, watch TV.
Give in—Don't insist on winning arguments all the time.
Do something for someone else.
Have some fun—Find a hobby, sport, or other interest.
Make a priority list—Do the most important jobs first.
Don't be self-critical.

---

1. Which of these tips do you think would be helpful for university students?
2. What ways have you found to relieve stress due to academic pressures?
3. Write a paragraph for the Health Services pamphlet.
   Topic Sentence: Introduce the enumeration of ways to relieve stress. This sentence can be a statement or a question.
   Support: Select the four most effective tips from questions 1 and 2 above. Use these tips and any explanations necessary to support your topic sentence. Introduce each tip with a discourse marker for enumerating.
   Concluding Sentence: Reformulate your topic sentence.

Exercise 4 Write Your Own Paragraph

Choose *one* of the following topics.

1. Write a paragraph for the university's orientation pamphlet for new students, enumerating ways to improve their study habits.
2. The university is going to double foreign students' tuition fees. You are against this decision. Write a letter to the student newspaper enumerating the reasons for disagreeing with the university's decision.
3. A new television station is being planned in your city. You think there should be no advertising on this station. Write a letter to the person responsible for programming; give your opinion and enumerate the disadvantages of advertising.
4. You are either the inventor of a new device or the manufacturer of a new product. You are writing an article introducing it to the public. Write the paragraph which enumerates the advantages or benefits of your invention or product. (*Note:* if you choose this topic, you have to "create" the device or product before you begin to write!)

5. You are a doctor who writes a weekly column in your city's newspaper. This week you are writing about an illness or a disease. Decide on an illness or disease and write the paragraph which enumerates the symptoms.
6. Choose your own topic; decide on the audience and purpose. Write a paragraph of enumeration.

EXAM-TYPE QUESTIONS

Certain examination questions require you to *list* or *give* reasons, causes, purposes, etc. The paragraph organization you have practiced in this chapter is suitable for such questions.

Give three major characteristics of (the mammal) and briefly explain each characteristic.

Your topic sentence would be a statement of enumeration, using the relevant words from the question.

        There are three major characteristics of the mammal.
or   **Mammals have three major characteristics.**

Then support your topic sentence with the three characteristics and a brief explanation of each. Introduce each characteristic with an appropriate discourse marker. Write a suitable concluding sentence.

Your teacher will give you practice with this type of question related to your reading or your own field of study (see Teacher's Notes, page 109).

4

COMPARISON I: TALKING ABOUT DIFFERENCES

We make comparisons every day—whenever we consider similarities and differences:

The weather here is the same as the weather at home.
The cost of food at this store is higher than the cost at that one.
This student is learning English faster than that one.

In the next two chapters, you will learn how to write sentences and then paragraphs which compare and contrast information.

SENTENCES

Exercise 1

Read the following information.
Most students have to compare and contrast available housing possibilities. A student called for information about the apartments in the following advertisements. He jotted down a few points about each apartment during his phone conversation.

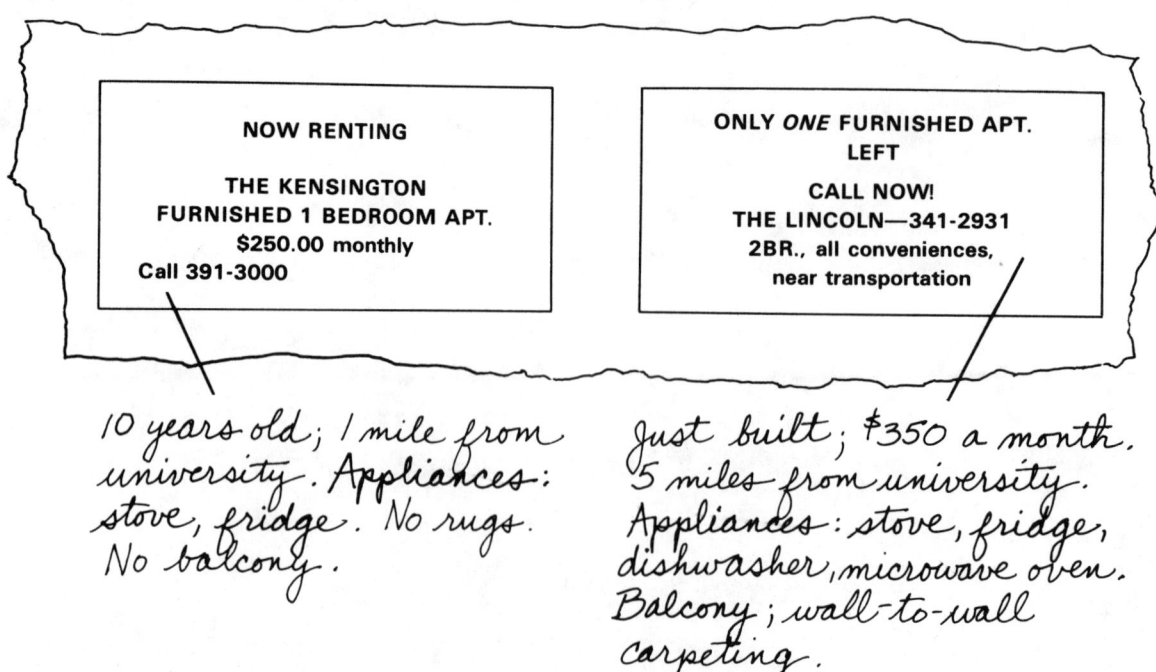

Discourse Markers for Expressing Contrast: Group A

Coordinator	Subordinators	Adverbial connectives
But	Whereas While Although	However On the other hand

Note: (1) *Although* implies that the contrast is surprising or unexpected. Use *although* for contrast, only if you want to make this implication. (2) *Whereas* is formal. (3) Use *on the other hand* when "on the one hand ... on the other hand" is implied.

Exercise 2 Using Group A Discourse Markers

The following sentences can be joined using each of the three kinds of discourse markers in Group A.

Consider the information about carpeting in the two apartments.

The Kensington has no rugs.   **The Lincoln has wall-to-wall carpeting.**

Coordinator
The Kensington has no rugs *but* The Lincoln has wall-to-wall carpeting.

Subordinator
While The Kensington has no rugs, The Lincoln has wall-to-wall carpeting.

Adverbial Connective
The Kensington has no rugs; *however*, The Lincoln has wall-to-wall carpeting.

Note: However can also be placed at the end of the sentence or after the subject. At the end of the sentence it is preceded by a comma. When it is placed after the subject, it has commas before and after it.

Link these sentences expressing contrast with the kinds of discourse marker indicated.

The Lincoln is 5 miles from the university.   The Kensington is only 1 mile away.

1. Coordinator _____

   _____

2. Subordinator _____

   _____

3. Adverbial connective _____

   _____

COMPARISON I: DIFFERENCES: Sentences

Discourse Markers for Expressing Contrast: Group B

Verbs and verb phrases	Comparative adjectives/adverbs	Prepositions	Noun
Pattern 1: A { contrasts with / is unlike / is different from / differs from } B	(tall)er than . . . more / less { (important) than	Unlike A, B In contrast to A, B	One / The } difference (between A and B)
Pattern 2: A and B are different			

Exercise 3 *Using Group B Discourse Markers*

A. VERB PHRASES Consider the information about the two apartments. Are they, on the whole, similar or different? Verb phrases from the chart above are useful when you are making a statement about differences in general.

The Kensington *is different from* The Lincoln.

1. Use three other verb phrases from the chart and write sentences which state that the two apartments differ.

    a. _____

    b. _____

    c. _____

    When you want to be specific about what the difference is, use one of the verb phrases plus *regarding* or *with respect to* and name the difference.

    The Kensington and The Lincoln differ *regarding/with respect to* rent.

2. Rewrite your sentences from number 1 using *with respect to* or *regarding* and a specific feature that is different in the apartments.

    a. _____

    b. _____

    c. _____

B. COMPARATIVE ADJECTIVES Consider the rent in the two apartments.

The Kensington is cheap*er than* The Lincoln.
The Lincoln is *more* expensive *than* The Kensington.

Write a statement of contrast about the following features of the two apartments. Use comparative adjectives.

1. Size (use *big* or *large*) _____

   _____

2. Age (use *old*) _____

   _____

3. Distance from the university (use *close* or *far*) _____

   _____

C. PREPOSITIONS   Consider the number of bedrooms in the two apartments. The Kensington has one; The Lincoln has two.

   Unlike The Kensington, The Lincoln has two bedrooms.

Use phrases with the preposition *unlike* to write statements of contrast about the following features of the two apartments.

1. Balcony _____

2. Rugs _____

3. A microwave oven and a dishwasher _____

   _____

D. NOUN

   One *difference* between The Lincoln and The Kensington is the rent.

Use the noun *difference* to write a statement contrasting one feature of The Kensington with one feature of The Lincoln.

_____

_____

Exercise 4   Guided Sentence Writing

Read the advertisements on the next page. Write sentences of contrast based on the information in these advertisements. Use appropriate discourse markers from the group indicated.

44 COMPARISON I: DIFFERENCES: Sentences

PRINCE GEORGE SCHOOL

An excellent education for your son and daughter
Ages: 6–18

Never more than 500 students at the school.

Your child lives at home—with you—and learns with us!

CALL 932-4000

QRS QUEENSTOWN RESIDENTIAL SCHOOL FOR BOYS

During the important developmental years, 6–12, your son will live at school, among 250 other children.

Excellent staff.
Excellent facilities.

For more information
Call 621-6413

1. *Group A Discourse Markers*

   a. (where the students live) _____

   _____

   b. (sex of students) _____

   _____

2. *Group B Discourse Markers*

   a. (size—large/small) _____

   _____

   b. (age of students—old/young) _____

   _____

Exercise 5 Writing Sentences of Contrast

Read the following report from a magazine comparing two cars. Then use the information in the chart to write sentences of contrast. Use a variety of discourse markers from Group A and Group B.

	Model	
	SX100	SX500
Size of car	2 door	4 door
Size of engine	4 cylinder	6 cylinder
Miles per gallon	25	19
Noise level	Very noisy	Moderately noisy
Comfort	Comfortable in front; uncomfortable in rear	Comfortable in front and rear
Repairs	Few repairs were needed in first year	Many repairs were needed in first year

1. _____
2. _____
3. _____
4. _____
5. _____

Exercise 6 Write Your Own Sentences

Write your own sentences expressing contrast about any topic. Use appropriate discourse markers.

1. _____
2. _____
3. _____
4. _____
5. _____

PARAGRAPHS

Exercise 1

A. From the list below choose an area of interest to you. You will be investigating two representatives or examples from this area in order to compare them for similarities and differences.

Restaurants or cafeterias on or off campus	Minicomputers
Libraries or reading rooms on campus	Cameras
Food stores in this city	Cars
Bookstores in this city	Insurance policies
Record shops in this city	Bank accounts
Pubs in this city	Theaters in this city
TV sets	Entertainment subscriptions available in this
Tape recorders	city for drama, music, or films
Typewriters	Travel packages
Word processors	Other

Now form a group with others who have chosen the same area of interest as you have (see Teacher's Notes, page 111).

B. In order to find similarities and differences, you must have bases or grounds for comparison. For example, if you were investigating clothing stores, you could develop a chart something like this:

Bases of comparison	Store 1	Store 2
1. Kind of store:		
Discount		
Department		
Specialty		
Used clothes		
2. For whom:		
Men		
Women		
Children		
3. Kinds of clothes:		
Sports		
Coats, jackets		
Dresses/suits		
Sweaters		
Blouses/shirts		
Underwear		
Socks		
Shoes, boots		
4. Price range		
5. Size of shop		
6. Atmosphere:		
Staff		
Helpful		
Unavailable		
Overly present		
Music		
Present		
Not present		
Too loud		
7. Location:		
Buses		
Parking		
8. Hours/days of operation		

With your teacher and the rest of the class, list as many bases of comparison as you can for hotels.

C. Now, work with your group: find as many bases of comparison as you can for the area you chose. Check these with your teacher when you are finished. Your teacher will then help you select two specific places (stores, restaurants, etc.) to visit in order to gather your data.

D. For homework, visit the places decided on and fill out a chart like the one above. Bring your information back to class.

COMPARISON I: DIFFERENCES: Paragraphs

Exercise 2 Read and Analyze

A. Two different patterns of organization are commonly used in writing comparisons. The following memos illustrate these patterns.
   1. Read the memo below, written by an accommodation officer for the College Student Housing Office.

Memo

To: J. M. Brown, Student Housing Office

From: Philip Patterson

Re: Available student accommodation

(1) The Varsity and Towers were checked this morning (August 27) and compared regarding age, rent, facilities, etc. (2) The two apartments are quite different. (3) The Varsity is new and therefore clean and in excellent condition. (4) The rent is $300 per month. (5) Facilities include a pool, sauna, party room, laundry room, and access to golf and tennis. (6) Neither children nor pets are allowed so the building is quiet. (7) The Towers, on the other hand, is fifteen years old. (8) As a result, it is getting run-down although it is very clean. (9) The rent is lower than the rent at The Varsity: $200 compared with $300. (10) There are fewer facilities at The Towers, just a laundry room and party room. (11) Unlike The Varsity, The Towers allows children and pets; as a result, the building is noisier. (12) I believe both buildings are suitable for our students; budget and tolerance of noise would be determining factors in apartment selection.

---

   2. Sentences 1 and 2 together introduce the paragraph.
      a. Which sentence tells you the paragraph will compare apartments?
      b. Which tells you if the apartments are similar or different?
   3. Which apartment are sentences 3 through 6 about?
   4. Which apartment are sentences 7 through 11 about?
   5. What discourse marker in sentence 7 indicates the change from one apartment to the other?
   6*a.* Underline the features of the apartment considered in sentences 3 through 6.
     b. Underline the features considered in sentences 7 through 11.
     c. These features are the bases of comparison. Are these bases considered in the same order or a different order for each apartment?
   7. Circle the discourse markers which express contrast.
   8. Find the discourse markers which express result.
   9. The concluding sentence is a recommendation. What is this recommendation?
   10. What is the purpose of the memo?

48 COMPARISON I: DIFFERENCES: Paragraphs

Format for Writing Paragraphs of Contrast: Pattern 1

Topic sentence(s): introduce(s) and state(s) the contrast

Support:

Subject 1:	a. Age → condition	
Bases of comparison:	b. Rent	
(The Varsity)	c. Facilities	
	d. Children and pets → noise	
Subject 2:	a. Age → condition	
Bases of comparison:	b. Rent	Discourse markers
(The Towers)	c. Facilities	for contrast
	d. Children and pets → noise	

Concluding sentence: a recommendation, summary, statement, etc., as required

---

B. The same memo could be organized differently.

> **Memo**
>
> To: J. M. Brown, Student Housing Office
> From: Philip Patterson
> Re: Available Student Accommodation
>
> (1) The Varsity and Towers were checked this morning (August 27) and compared regarding age, rent, facilities, etc. (2) The two apartments are quite different. (3) The Varsity is new and therefore clean and in excellent condition; The Towers, on the other hand, is fifteen years old and starting to get run-down, although it, too, is very clean. (4) The rent at The Varsity is higher than the rent at The Towers: $300 compared with $200. (5) While The Varsity has many facilities (a pool, sauna, party room, laundry room, access to tennis and golf), The Towers has only a laundry room and party room. (6) The two apartments also differ regarding children and pets. (7) The Varsity doesn't allow them and The Towers does. (8) As a result, The Varsity is quieter than The Towers. (9) I believe both buildings are suitable for our students; budget and tolerance of noise would be determining factors in apartment selection.

1. The topic and concluding sentences are the same as those in Pattern 1. Read sentences 3, 4, 5, 6, 7, and 8, and decide which basis of comparison is considered in each. Which apartment is considered in each?
2. Underline the discourse markers indicating contrast.
3. Explain the use of *although* in sentence 3.

COMPARISON I: DIFFERENCES: Paragraphs   49

Format for Writing Paragraphs of Contrast: Pattern 2

Topic sentence(s): introduce(s) and state(s) contrast

Support:
   Bases of comparison:
     a. Age → condition: Subject 1 (The Varsity)
                                 Subject 2 (The Towers)
     b. Rent   Subject 1
                                       Subject 2   Discourse markers
     c. Facilities   Subject 1   for contrast
                                       Subject 2
     d. Children and pets → noise   Subject 1
                                       Subject 2

Concluding sentence: a recommendation, summary statement, etc., as required

Exercise 3   *Class Composition*

Do this exercise with your teacher and class using the board to build your paragraph together.

1. Compare the information below about the restaurant and cafeteria. On the whole, are they similar or different?

Bases of comparison	Residence restaurant	Student union cafeteria
Food	Salad bar Custom sandwich bar Daily hot special Ethnic specialty Freshly baked cakes and pies	Fish and chips Hamburgers Hot dogs Packaged sandwiches Packaged cookies and doughnuts
Price range	$1.50–$4.00	$0.95–$2.00
Beverages	Wine, beer Soft drinks Juices Coffee, tea, milk	Soft drinks Juices Coffee, tea, milk
Decor and atmosphere	Dim lights Dividers partition the room into small, private sections Quiet Carpeting	Bright, bustling Many windows One large open room

2. Write a paragraph comparing the two places.
   Topic Sentence: Based on your answer to question 1, write a topic sentence in which you name the two restaurants and state that they are similar/different.
   Support: Support your topic sentence with information from the chart. Use Pattern 1. Then reorganize your support using Pattern 2. Introduce your sentences of contrast with appropriate discourse markers.
   Concluding Sentence: Make a recommendation to (1) a student on a limited budget; (2) a student who wants to take his girlfriend out for lunch on her birthday.

Exercise 4 Guided Writing

Do either A or B. Use either Pattern 1 or Pattern 2 to organize your paragraph.

A. Use the information you gathered in Exercise 1, Paragraphs.
1. If you investigated restaurants, libraries, food stores, bookstores, record shops, or pubs, write a paragraph for new students or people new to the area to tell them about the differences in the two places you visited.
Topic Sentence(s): Name the two places you visited and state that they are different.
Support: Support your topic sentence with the information you gathered. Examine each basis of comparison and give examples or explanations to reinforce the points you are making. Use discourse markers for expressing contrast.
Concluding Sentence: Recommend the place you prefer and explain (briefly) why you prefer it.
2. If you chose one of the other topics, your audience is the general public, and your purpose is to contrast the two items.
Topic Sentence: Name the items compared and state that they are different.
Support: Support your topic sentence with the information you gathered. Examine each basis of comparison and give examples or explanations to reinforce the points you are making. Use discourse markers for expressing contrast.
Concluding Sentence: State which item you think is better or preferable and (briefly) tell why.

B. (See Teacher's Notes, page 111.) Work with a partner from another country which is very different from yours. Interview each other about education in each of your countries. Consider:
1. The cost: Is it free? If not, who pays—parents? the government?
2. The divisions (elementary? secondary? post-secondary? What are the ages in each level?).
3. The amount of freedom (*a*) in attending school (Is education compulsory? If yes, until what age?), (*b*) in subject choices (Are subjects compulsory? Can students choose their courses?).

After you have interviewed your partner, write a paragraph for the students in your class to contrast the two systems of education.
Topic Sentence: Name the two countries whose education system you are discussing and state that they are, on the whole, different.
Support: Support your topic sentence with information from your interview. Examine each basis of comparison and give specific details to reinforce your point. Use discourse markers for expressing contrast.
Concluding Sentence: Write a sentence which either (1) summarizes briefly the content of the paragraph or (2) reformulates the topic sentence.

Exercise 5 Write Your Own Paragraph (see Teacher's Notes, page 111)

Choose *one* of the following:
1. You are a journalist for a newspaper in your country. You have agreed to write a series of articles contrasting aspects of life in your country and in another. (If you are a foreign student, contrast the city where you are studying to your own city.) Write a paragraph of contrast about *one* of the following:

Customs	Recreational activities	Music
Food	Role of women	Superstitions
Fashions	Religion	
Lifestyle	Weather	

2. You are writing a section of a high school science textbook. Write a paragraph in which you contrast *one* of the following:

        Two insects   Two animals
        Two birds   Two plants

3. You are a free-lance writer for a popular student magazine. Write a paragraph in which you contrast *one* of the following:

        A simple computer and a calculator
        Two TV shows of the same type (e.g., comedy, game show)
        Two albums (early and recent) by a popular singer/musician

4. Your own topic.

EXAM-TYPE QUESTIONS

When you are asked to *compare*, on an exam, you are generally expected to give similarities and differences. When you are asked to *contrast*, give differences only.

Contrast the characteristics of mammals and reptiles.

Your topic sentence should be a generalization which states that there are differences between the two types (items, etc.) being compared.

        Mammals and reptiles have several differences.
or   **Mammals and reptiles differ in several respects.**

Then support your topic sentence; decide on the bases of comparison and organize your information according to Pattern 1 or Pattern 2. Use appropriate discourse markers for expressing contrast. Conclude the paragraph with a sentence which either sums up the content or restates the topic sentence.

Your teacher will give you examples of this type of question based on your reading or your field of study.

5
COMPARISON II: TALKING ABOUT SIMILARITIES

SENTENCES

Exercise 1

Read these notes made by a student looking for accommodation:

```
The Kent                          The Lionsgate
- rent - $400                     - rent - $350
- 3 miles from university         - 5 miles from university
- furnished                       - furnished
- has washing machines            - has washing machines
  in basement                     - pool, sauna, party room
- recreational facilities:        - doesn't permit
  pool, sauna, party room             - children
- it doesn't allow                    - pets
  children                        - parking included in
- it doesn't allow pets             rent
- doesn't charge extra            - 12 month lease
  for parking                     - has a bus stop on
- requires 1 year lease             the corner
- is close to                     - 15 stories
  transportation
- 15 floors
```

Discourse Markers for Expressing Similarity: Group A

Adverbial connectives

Likewise
Similarly

Note: *Similarly* and *likewise* are quite formal.

Exercise 2   Using Group A Discourse Markers

Consider the charge for parking in the two apartments in Exercise 1. We can say:

The Kent doesn't charge extra for parking; ***similarly*****, The Lionsgate includes parking in the rent.**

Write a sentence about the proximity of transportation to the two apartments. Use an adverbial connective to show similarity.

___

___

Discourse Markers for Expressing Similarity: Group B

Verbs or verb phrases	Preposition	Correlative conjunctions	Determiners/pronouns
Pattern 1: A { is the same as / is like / is similar to / resembles } B Pattern 2: A and B { are the same / are alike / are similar }	Like A, B	Both . . . and Neither . . . nor	Both Neither

Exercise 3   Using Group B Discourse Markers

A. VERBS AND VERB PHRASES   The terms *the same as, like, the same,* and *alike* refer to sameness. *Similar to, resembles,* and *are similar* refer to similarity. The verb and verb phrases in the chart above are useful when you are making a statement about similarity or sameness in general.

The Lionsgate *is similar to* The Kent.

1. Use a verb phrase from each of Pattern 1 and Pattern 2 and write sentences which state that the two apartments are similar.

a. ___

b. ___

When you want to be specific about what features are similar, use the verb phrases, add *regarding* or *with respect to*, and name the feature.

The Kent and The Lionsgate are similar *regarding* parking.

2. Rewrite sentences *a* and *b*. This time be specific about a feature which is similar or the same in the apartments. Use *regarding* or *with respect to* to introduce the feature.

a. ___

b. ___

54 COMPARISON II: SIMILARITIES: Sentences

B. PREPOSITIONS Consider the recreational facilities. The Kent has a party room, sauna, and pool. The Lionsgate has these features too.

> *Like* The Lionsgate, The Kent has a party room, sauna, and pool.

Use the pattern above, and write statements of similarity about the following features in the two apartments.

1. Washing machines _____

2. Lease _____

C. CORRELATIVE CONJUNCTIONS: *Affirmative—Both ... and*   Consider the following.

The Kent is furnished.   **The Lionsgate is furnished.**
Both **The Kent** *and* **The Lionsgate are furnished.**

1. Use *both ... and* to write sentences of similarity about the following features:

   a. Pool, sauna, party room _____

   _____

   b. Number of floors in the building _____

   _____

   Negative—Neither ... nor

   The Kent does*n't* allow pets.   **The Lionsgate does*n't* allow pets.**
   Neither **The Kent** *nor* **The Lionsgate allows pets.**

   Note: The negative idea is presented by *neither ... nor*. No other negative is needed in the sentence.

2. Use *neither ... nor* to write statements about the following:

   a. Children _____

   b. Parking _____

Exercise 4 Writing Sentences of Similarity

Read the information below from a report comparing models of cassette recorders.

	Model 2567	Model 3000
Price	$49.50	$49.50
Weight	4¼ pounds	4 pounds
Tone	Good	Excellent
Features:		
Power control	+	+
Tone control	+	+
Fast forward	+	+
Rewind	+	+
Tape counter	−	−
Record meter	−	−
Record light	−	−

+ indicates presence of feature.
− indicates absence of feature.

Based on the information above, write sentences expressing *similarity*. Use appropriate discourse markers.

1. _____
2. _____
3. _____
4. _____
5. _____

Exercise 5 Write Your Own Sentences

Write your own sentences of similarity about any topic. Use appropriate discourse markers.

1. _____
2. _____
3. _____
4. _____
5. _____

PARAGRAPHS

Exercise 1 Read and Analyze

1. Read the following memo comparing two rooming houses.

Memo

To: J. M. Brown, Student Housing Office

From: Philip Patterson

Re: Available student accommodation

(1) Two more housing possibilities were investigated, The Co-op Rooming House and Mrs. Whyte's. (2) They are, on the whole, alike. (3) The rent is the same: $40 per week. (4) The rooms in both places are tiny, with only a minimum of furniture: a bed, small dresser, and a table/desk. (5) Both the Co-op and Mrs. Whyte's are in bad condition; the houses appear neglected and dirty. (6) Neither the Co-op nor Mrs. Whyte's has adequate cooking or bathroom facilities. (7) One difference between the two is that the Co-op provides a TV room for the residents. (8) Because the houses are in poor condition and the facilities are so inadequate, I cannot recommend either of these rooming houses; in fact, I suggest we remove them from our student housing list.

2a. What is the general topic, as given in sentence 1?
 b. According to sentence 2, what specific point of view or direction will the paragraph develop?
3. Underline the bases of comparison mentioned in sentences 3, 4, 5, and 6.
4. Is the information organized according to Pattern 1 or Pattern 2? (Chapter 4)
5. Circle the discourse markers which indicate similarity.
6. According to sentence 8, what conclusion does Mr. Patterson reach about the two rooming houses?
7. What is the purpose of this memo?

Note: Use Pattern 2 for writing paragraphs about similarity.

Exercise 2 Class Composition

Do this exercise with your teacher and class, using the blackboard to build your paragraph together.

1. Read the information about the broadcast journalism programs offered by two colleges. As you read, consider whether the two programs are the same or different regarding entrance requirements, length of program, cost, and degree on graduation.

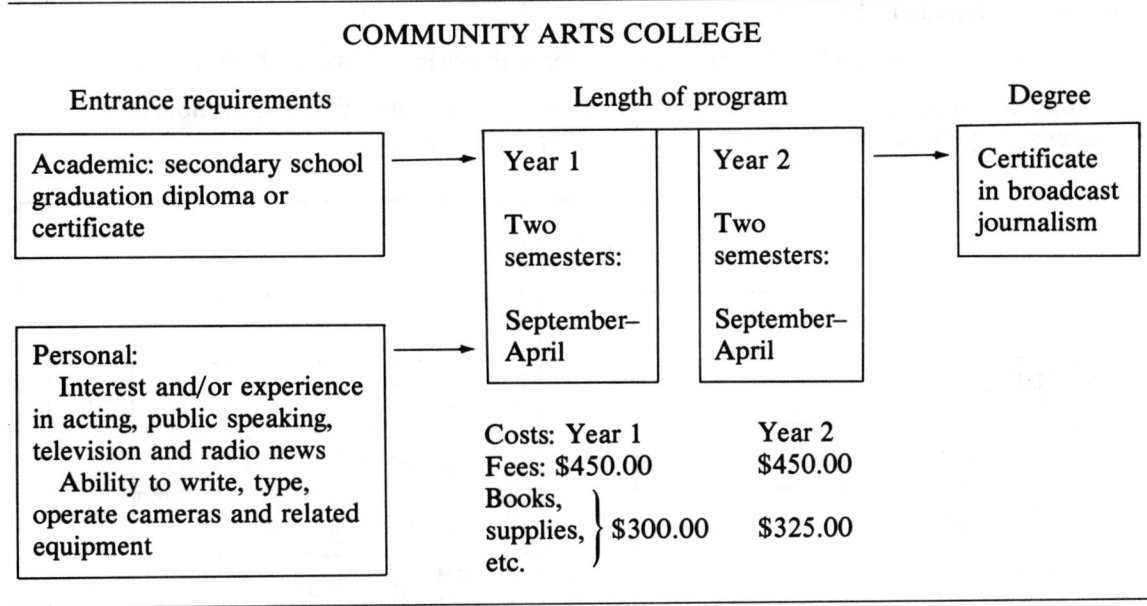

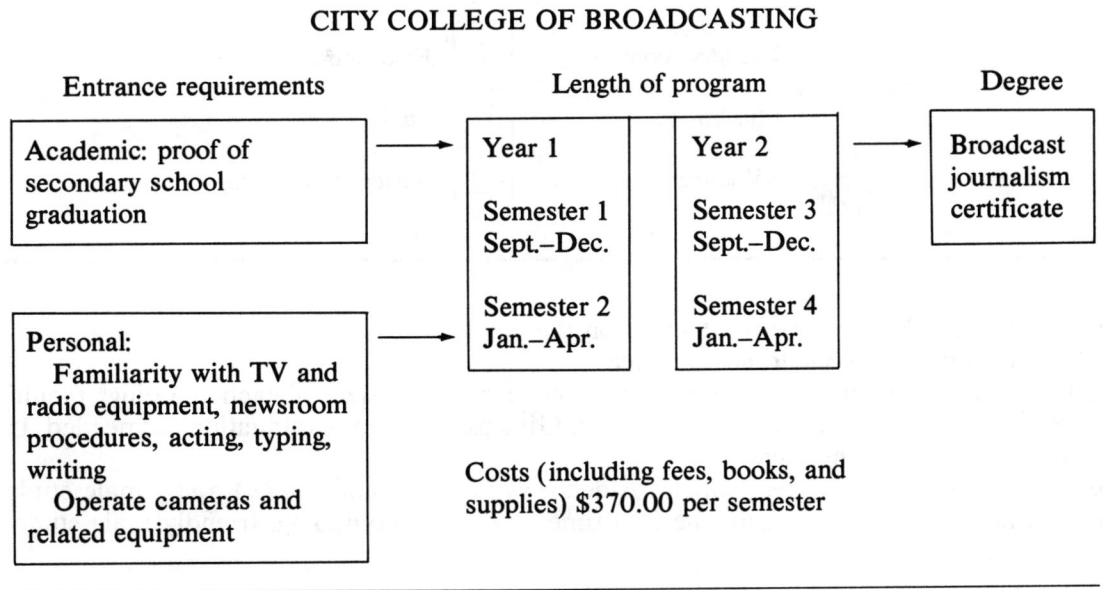

2. Write a paragraph comparing the two programs for prospective students.
   Topic Sentence(s): State that the Community Arts College and the City College of Broadcasting offer broadcast journalism programs and state whether the programs are, on the whole, similar or different.
   Support: Support your topic sentence(s) by discussing these bases of comparison: entrance requirements, length of program, total cost for the two-year program, and degree on graduation. Use appropriate discourse markers.
   Concluding Sentence: Since the two programs have so much in common, recommend them equally.

58 COMPARISON II: SIMILARITIES: Paragraphs

Exercise 3 Guided Writing

Choose either A or B. Use the format for comparing, Pattern 2, page 49.

A. You are an adviser for first-year students at a university. Write a comparison of two residences at your university based on the information below.

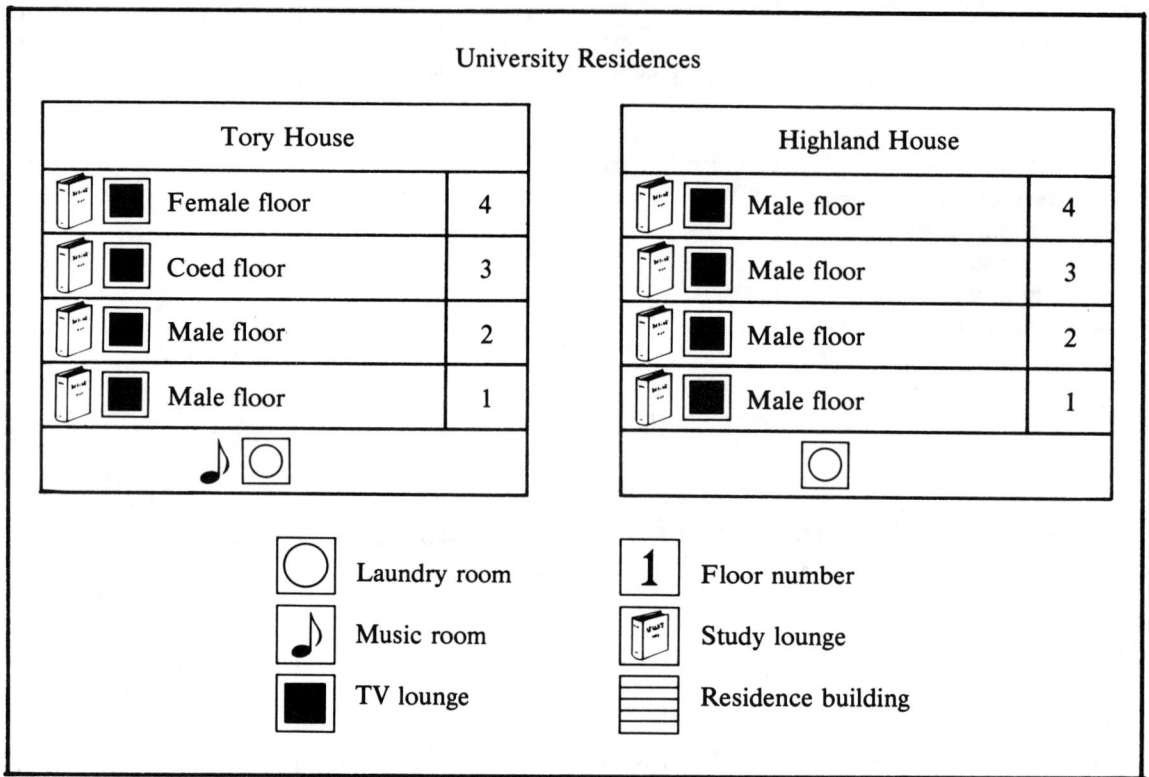

Topic Sentence: Are the two residences, on the whole, similar or different? Your answer to this question will be your topic sentence.

Support: Support your topic sentence by considering the size of each building, facilities available in each, and the sex of the residents. Give examples or explanations as needed. Use appropriate discourse markers.

Concluding Sentence: Suggest which residence is most suitable for (*a*) a shy male student who will be away from home for the first time, and (*b*) an outgoing, friendly male student.

B. You write about holidays for a travel magazine. You have received these pamphlets about two resort towns.

VISIT Belmont-on-the-lake

Accommodation: Beautiful campgrounds overlooking the lake, reasonable motels, luxurious hotels.

Food: Variety! That's what you'll find at Belmont. Ethnic foods, outdoor barbecues, fresh fish— or shop at our outdoor market, pack a picnic, and enjoy the countryside around the lake.

Recreation: Something for everyone: tennis, golf, fishing, sailing, canoeing, water skiing—or just relaxing on the beach.

Entertainment: Choose from nightly performances of live theater, symphony concerts, dance companies, or folk/jazz in the parks. And don't miss the arts and crafts exhibits along the boardwalk.

See you in Belmont!

60 COMPARISON II: SIMILARITIES: Paragraphs

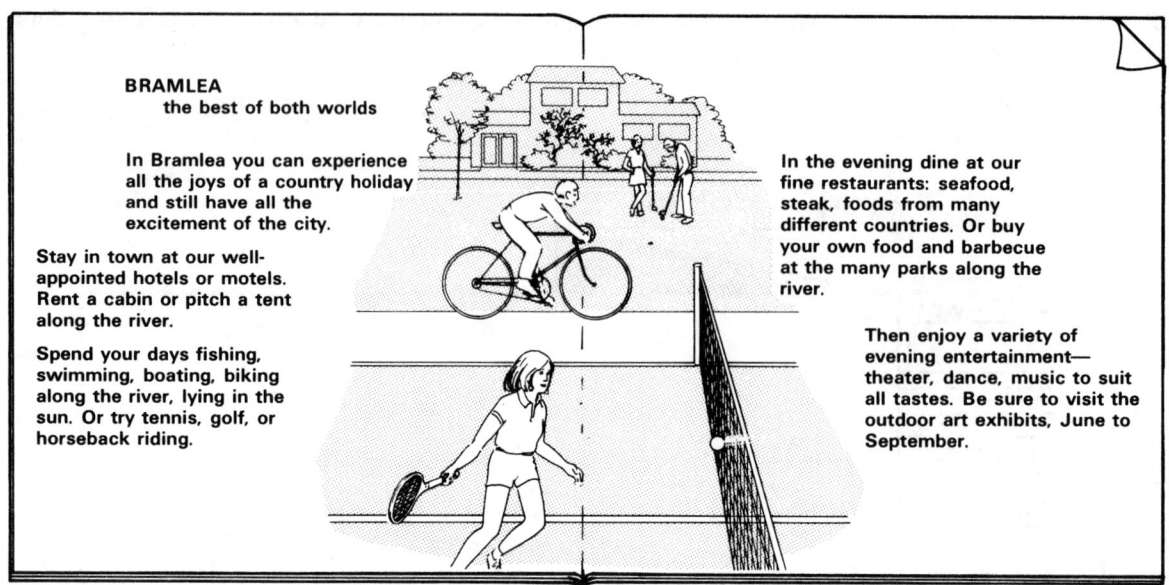

After visiting the two towns, you have found that the information in the pamphlets is accurate.

Write a paragraph for your magazine in which you show the similarities between the two towns. Use Pattern 2.

Topic Sentence(s): (*a*) Name the two towns and state that they are similar, or (*b*) ask the readers if they have ever visited the two towns. Then, in the next sentence, state that they are similar.

Support: Support your topic sentence by referring to the similarities in entertainment, accommodation, recreation, and food. Be specific. Use appropriate discourse markers for similarity.

Concluding Sentence: Recommend both places and briefly state why.

Exercise 4   Write Your Own Paragraph (see Teacher's Notes, page 112)

Choose *one* of the following.

1. Exercise 5, number 1, page 50. Write about similarities instead of contrasts.
2. Exercise 5, number 2, page 51. Write about similarities instead of contrasts.
3. You are a free-lance writer for a popular student magazine. You are writing a review on *one* of the following:

    Two television shows of the same type (e.g., comedy, game show)
    Two musicians
    Two restaurants
    Two films

    Write the paragraph which points out the similarities between the two shows, musicians, restaurants, or films.
4. Your own topic.

EXAM-TYPE QUESTIONS

Certain examination questions require a discussion of similarities. The question will include the word *similarities* or *similar*.

What are the similarities between a calculator and a computer?

Your topic sentence should state that the two topics, items, etc., are similar.

Calculators and computers are similar in many ways.

Decide on the similarities; then support your topic sentence with this information. Use Pattern 2 and appropriate discourse markers. Write a suitable concluding sentence.

If the exam question says, "Compare A and B," you will probably have to write at least two paragraphs—one for similarities and one for differences. Use appropriate organization and discourse markers for each paragraph.

Your teacher will give you examples of questions like these based on your reading and your field of study.

6

DEFINITION

We need definitions whenever we want to make an unfamiliar term clear. When specific terminology is necessary in your writing and the audience is laymen, defining or explaining your terms is very important.

In this chapter you will learn how to write both informal and formal definitions.

SENTENCES

Exercise 1

A. Work with your teacher and class and try to give the meanings of these words:

        Friendship
        Neurotic
        Xenophobia

B. Do this part of the exercise alone. Find the meanings of the following words by consulting a good English-English dictionary.

Word	Definition
Desalinization	
Alloy	
Calipers	
Podiatrist	

C. Do this part of the exercise for homework. Ask people to help you with the meanings of the words below by writing definitions in the space provided. (Your teacher and your class may want to add words for defining to the list.) In Exercise 6 we will return to this exercise and discuss the kinds of definitions used.

Word	Definition
1. I'm *fed up*	
2. He's *uptight*	
3. She's *hung up*	
4. A numismatist	
5. Anthropology	
6.	
7.	

INFORMAL DEFINITIONS

Sometimes we define a term by explaining it. There are several ways to do this.

You can use a synonym; e.g., An *ophthalmologist* is an eye doctor.

You can explain the unknown word or concept. The explanation is often introduced by the following discourse markers.

Discourse Markers for Explaining
Adverbial connectives
That is (to explain) In other words (to explain by reformulating)

Examples

> Many people suffer from *insomnia*; *that is*, they cannot sleep.
> Many people suffer from *insomnia*; *in other words*, they cannot sleep.

You can place a synonym or an explanation between dashes, between commas, or in parentheses.

> *Bulimia*—the binge-eating syndrome—affects women in their 20s and 30s and seems to be brought on by stress.
>
> *Bulimia*, the binge-eating syndrome, affects women in their 20s and 30s and seems to be brought on by stress.
>
> *Bulimia* (the binge-eating syndrome) affects women in their 20s and 30s and seems to be brought on by stress.

Exercise 2

In the following sentences (*a*) What does the italicized word mean? (*b*) What method is used to define or explain the word?

1. *Amniocentesis* (a test for genetic defects in a fetus) has caused a great deal of controversy because of its influence on abortions of deformed babies.
2. The first-year music class is studying the *concerto*—a musical composition for one or more solo instruments and orchestra.
3. Morphine is an *analgesic;* in other words, it is one of the drugs used to relieve pain.
4. Certain drugs are *depressants;* that is, they make you sad.
5. The groom's parents were angry because the bride's *dowry*—her money and property—was small.

64   DEFINITION: Sentences

Exercise 3   Guided Writing

A. Define the italicized words in the sentences below by rewriting the sentence and including the synonym or explanation on the right. Put the synonym or explanation between commas, between dashes, or in parentheses.

1. *Manual laborers* often get very low wages.   People who work with their hands

_____

2. Everyone would be *annihilated* in a nuclear war.   Totally destroyed

_____

3. Some people don't have the *capacity* to learn languages; others can't learn mathematics.   The ability

_____

4. *Neurotransmitters* carry messages between the nerve cells and the brain.   Brain chemicals like serotonin

_____

B. Use *in other words* or *that is* to join the following sentences.

1. Many children *resemble* their parents. They are like them in looks, personality, or behavior.

_____

2. People who go without sleep for many days may become *paranoic*. They may think people are trying to harm them.

_____

3. Some pills *depress* heart action and respiration. These pills reduce the rate of the heartbeat and of breathing.

   _____
   _____

4. Some governments are very hard on *dissidents;* they deal harshly with people who disagree with their policies.

   _____
   _____

Exercise 4   Write Your Own Informal Definitions

Write sentences of your own in which you define either the following words or words of your own.

   Gregarious
   Contaminated
   Mechanize
   Facilities

1. _____
   _____

2. _____
   _____

3. _____
   _____

4. _____
   _____

FORMAL DEFINITIONS

Formal definitions give the meaning of an item by placing it within its class (or general category) and then giving the specific characteristics which make this item different from other members of that class.

66 DEFINITION: Sentences

Examples	Class	Characteristics
The pancreas is	a body organ	which lies crosswise behind the stomach and produces insulin.
Sociology is	a science	which studies society and social behavior.

Exercise 5

In the following definitions, (*a*) What is the class? (*b*) What are the characteristics?

1. A blender is an electrical appliance which makes a liquid out of solid foods.
2. A dehumidifier is a machine that takes moisture out of the air.
3. Blood is a red liquid which flows throughout the bodies of humans and higher animals.
4. A corkscrew is a gadget which is used to remove a cork from a wine bottle.
5. Sugar is a sweet substance that is obtained from the juices of plants such as sugar cane or sugar beet.

(Note the words in the preceding sentences used for class or category. Other such words are *device, tool, implement, utensil, instrument, process*.)

Exercise 6

Now look at your definitions from Exercise 1. Were the definitions you collected for Part C formal or informal? Were the definitions you found in the dictionary formal or informal?

Exercise 7 Sentence Combining

Combine the sentences below using the following subordinators:

Subordinators

Which—refers to things only
That—refers to things or people
Who—refers to people only

Note: These subordinators are used for combining sentences which have many different types of functions. Their use is *not* limited to sentences of definition.

The combined sentences you write will be formal definitions.

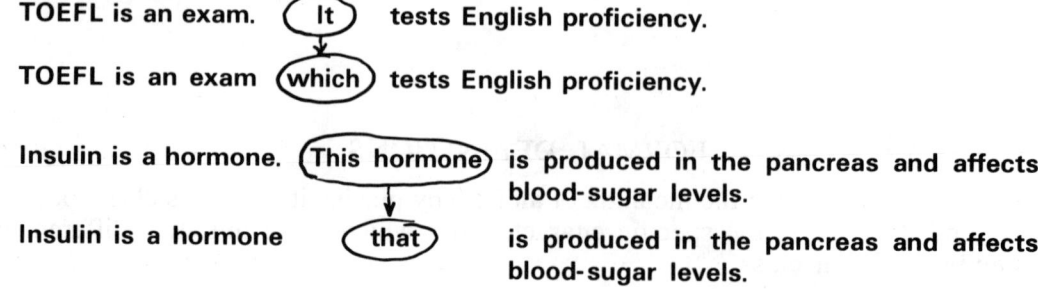

DEFINITION: Sentences   67

1. An aviator is a person. This person controls an aircraft of some sort.

   _____
   _____

2. A choir is a group of people. The people are trained to sing together.

   _____
   _____

3. Astronomy is defined as a science. This science studies the sun, stars, moon, and planets.

   _____
   _____

4. A transistor is a small electronic device. It is used in radios, hearing aids, computers, and other kinds of electronic apparatus.

   _____
   _____

5. The common cold is an infection. This infection affects the nose, throat, air passages, and lungs.

   _____
   _____

Exercise 8 *Write Your Own Formal Definitions*

A. Work alone or with a partner. Write formal definitions of the words below or of five words from your own discipline. You can consult a dictionary.

1. Archaeology _____

2. Evaporation _____

3. An optician _____

4. Oxygen _____

5. A calculator _____

B. Work alone or with a partner. Write a formal definition; then test your definition by reading it to the class *but* omit the word you are defining.

   A _____ is an instrument which doctors use to hear a patient's heartbeat.

Exercise 9 (Optional)   Write Your Own Definitions

Compile a personal or class dictionary of difficult words. The definitions can be formal, informal, or both.

PARAGRAPHS

Definitions are used in paragraphs together with examples, descriptions, causes, and results. You will be writing paragraphs which include definitions in later chapters.

EXAM-TYPE QUESTIONS

You may be asked to define terms. You can do this by using a sentence definition. In longer answers, you may be required to define and explain, or define and give examples. For these longer answers, you would write a paragraph beginning with a definition of the term and continuing with support by explanation or example.

Your teacher will give you examples of this type of question, referring to the materials you have been reading or studying.

7

CAUSE AND RESULT I: CAUSES

We are concerned about causes whenever we try to understand why something happens: the economy of a country is bad, a riot breaks out, there is a leak in a nuclear reactor, a new medicine doesn't work. We want to discover the causes.

We are concerned about results, effects, consequences when we want to know the outcome of something. What are the effects of a new drug? What will the results of acid rain be? What will the consequences for a town be if a nuclear reactor is built nearby? In all these instances we are looking for results.

In the next two chapters you will learn how to write sentences and then paragraphs about causes and results.

SENTENCES

Exercise 1

Work either in groups or with your class. From the results listed, select the one which is most interesting to you. Then write the causes for this result (see Teacher's Notes, page 113).

1. *Result:* Air pollution
   Causes:

   a. _____

   b. _____

   c. _____

   d. _____

2. *Result:* Insomnia
   Causes:

   a. _____

   b. _____

   c. _____

   d. _____

3. *Result:* There is an increase in violence in big cities.
   Causes:

   a. _____

70   CAUSE AND RESULT I: Sentences

  b. _____

  c. _____

  d. _____

4. *Result:* People smoke although they know smoking is unhealthy.
   Causes:

  a. _____

  b. _____

  c. _____

  d. _____

5. *Result:* More people are getting divorced.
   Causes:

  a. _____

  b. _____

  c. _____

  d. _____

6. *Result:* An effect or result (political, social, etc.) whose causes are of interest to your class.
   Causes:

  a. _____

  b. _____

  c. _____

  d. _____

**Discourse Markers for Expressing Cause:
Group A**

Subordinators

Because
Since

If

Note: Use *if* when a condition is involved.

CAUSE AND RESULT I: Sentences 71

Exercise 2 Using Group A Discourse Markers

One class wrote the following causes for people smoking despite evidence that tobacco and nicotine are harmful.

> **Causes**
> **They are addicted.**
> **They don't think of the consequences.**
> **They think it is sophisticated.**

You can write cause/result sentences using Group A discourse markers. Remember that for this kind of discourse marker the cause and result must be in sentence form.

> ***Because/Since*** **people are addicted, they smoke despite evidence that tobacco and nicotine are harmful.**

1. Use *because* and *since* to write two other sentences about the causes of smoking given above.

a. _____

b. _____

2. Consider the sentence examples from Exercise 1 which your teacher wrote on the board. Write sentences using subordinators to introduce the causes.

a. _____

b. _____

c. _____

Discourse Markers for Expressing Cause: Group B

Focus on cause		Focus on cause and result
Prepositions	Noun	Verbs and Verb Phrases
Because of, Due to, On account of, As a result of } + noun	A/the cause (of ____)	The cause is before these: X { causes, results in, produces, leads to, brings about } Y The cause is after these: Y { results from, is a result of, is caused by } X

Note: The cause (X) and the result (Y) are expressed in noun form.

72 CAUSE AND RESULT I: Sentences

Exercise 3 Using Group B Discourse Markers

One class interested in the environment wrote the following causes of air pollution.

Causes
Poisonous fumes from motor vehicles
Harmful particles from burned garbage
Harmful substances from furnaces
Smoke from factories
Fluorocarbons in aerosol cans
Fine dust from grinding, sanding, or polishing processes
Evaporation of gasolines, paint, and cleaning solvents

A. PREPOSITIONS When the cause is in noun form, you can use prepositions as the discourse marker to introduce the cause. Note that the result, *air pollution*, has been made into a sentence.

Cause	*Result*
Poisonous fumes from motor vehicles.	The air is polluted.

Because of poisonous fumes from motor vehicles, the air is polluted.

1. Use prepositions to write about two other causes of air pollution from the list above.

   a. _____

   b. _____

2. Now consider the causes in noun form which your teacher listed on the board in Exercise 1. Write two sentences using prepositions to express cause.

   a. _____

   b. _____

B. NOUNS The noun *cause* can also be used to indicate cause.

One ***cause*** (of air pollution) is fumes from motor vehicles.

CAUSE AND RESULT I: Sentences   73

1. Use the noun *cause* to write statements about two other causes of air pollution on page 72.

   a. _____

   b. _____

2. Now write two statements about the causes in noun form your teacher listed on the board in Exercise 1. Use the noun *cause* as the discourse marker.

   a. _____

   b. _____

C. VERBS AND VERB PHRASES   Verbs and verb phrases express cause and result.

> **Poisonous fumes from motor vehicles *produce* air pollution.**
> **Air pollution *results from* poisonous fumes from motor vehicles.**

Note: Both the cause and result are in noun form.

1. Use verbs or verb phrases to write statements about the causes of air pollution.

   a. _____

   b. _____

2. Now write two statements about the cause/result relationship you chose in Exercise 1. Use appropriate verbs or verb phrases as discourse markers. (Remember: the cause and result must be in noun form.)

   a. _____

   b. _____

CAUSE AND RESULT I: Sentences

Exercise 4 Guided Sentence Writing

Based on the following information about causes for the rising divorce rate in the United States, write cause and result sentences. Use the kind of discourse marker indicated.

1. *Subordinator*
   a. Divorce is becoming more acceptable.   The divorce rate is increasing.

   _____

   b. Many young people are not willing to stay in a marriage and try to make it work.   There are more divorces now than there were before.

   _____

2. *Preposition*
   a. The relaxation of divorce laws   More people apply for divorces.

   _____

   b. The reduction of the waiting period   More people apply for divorces.

   _____

3. *Verbs and Verb Phrases*
   a. Changes in divorce laws   A rise in the divorce rate

   _____

   b. The availability of free legal services   A rise in the divorce rate

   _____

4. *Noun*
   a. Changes in divorce laws

   _____

   b. The availability of free legal services

   _____

Exercise 5 Write Your Own Sentences

Write five cause and result sentences on any topic. Use the discourse markers you learned in this chapter.

1. _____

   _____

2. _____

   _____

CAUSE AND RESULT I: Paragraphs

3. _____

_____

4. _____

_____

5. _____

_____

PARAGRAPHS

Exercise 1 Read and Analyze

Read the following excerpt from a medical handbook.

> **What causes cancer? No one knows for sure, but most doctors and scientists believe there are different causes for the different forms of the disease. Working conditions may lead to cancer. For example, people who work in close contact with chemical compounds like arsenic or asbestos may develop cancer. People who work for long periods of time with X-rays or radioactive material may get leukemia or cancer of the skin, bone, or lungs. Smoking is another cause of cancer. Many experiments have shown that smoking can produce lung cancer as well as cancer of the mouth, larynx and esophagus, pancreas, and urinary bladder. Finally, viruses may cause cancer. Scientific research has shown that viruses bring about certain kinds of cancer in laboratory animals. Scientists are now trying to find out if this is true for humans as well. Although we don't have the answer yet, perhaps in the near future we will know what causes this disease.**

1. Sentences 1 and 2 introduce the topic. (*a*) What is the general topic stated in sentence 1? (Notice the use of a question.) (*b*) What additional information is given in sentence 2?
2. Fill out this outline based on the information in the body of the paragraph.

Cause 1: _____

   Example 1: _____

   Example 2: _____

   Kinds of cancer caused by this working condition:

   _____

   _____

76 CAUSE AND RESULT I: Paragraphs

Cause 2: _____

    Kinds of cancer related to this cause: _____

_____

Cause 3: _____

    Explanation of research: _____

_____

3. Concluding sentence: Note the use of a statement to reformulate the question in the topic sentence.
4. Reread the paragraph. (*a*) Underline the discourse markers expressing cause. (*b*) Circle the discourse markers introducing examples. (*c*) Put a square around discourse markers indicating enumeration.
5. Was this paragraph written for doctors or the lay reader?
6. What is the purpose of this paragraph?

Note: Paragraphs about causes usually also include examples and/or explanations. If the paragraph considers several causes, discourse markers for addition or enumeration are often used.

Format for Paragraphs about Causes

Topic sentence(s): a question and/or statement which present(s) the cause/result relationship. Your topic is the cause.

Support:
    Cause plus example and/or explanation ⎫
    Cause plus example and/or explanation ⎬ Appropriate discourse markers
    Cause plus example and/or explanation ⎭

Concluding sentence: depending on the purpose of the paragraph, the concluding sentence can be a summarizing statement, a reformulation of the topic sentence, a question, etc.

Exercise 2   *Class Composition*

1. Discuss: In your opinion, at what point does noise become unbearable or unpleasant? What causes the noises or sounds you consider excessive?

    Note: Noise pollution is a term that refers to noises which are excessive in intensity or duration. If people work where there is high-intensity noise or moderate-intensity noise for long periods of time, they can suffer physical damage (i.e., hearing loss).
2. Consider the chart on the next page.

Noise is measured in units called decibels. The chart shows the approximate decibel level from some sources of noise.

Sources

Jet plane taking off	150	
Jet plane (30 meters away)	140	
Rock music at close range	130	Possible damage to hearing
	120	Threshold of feeling (pain is experienced)
Motorcycles	110	
Riveting machines (9 meters away)	100	
Power lawn mower	90	
Screeching subway train		Annoying
Highway traffic	80	
Vacuum cleaner	70	
	60	
Residential street traffic	50	
	40	
	30	Acceptable
Purring cat	20	
	10	
	0	Threshold of audibility (sound can just be heard)

3. Imagine that you are writing a science textbook for high school students. (Therefore, your purpose is to present information clearly and objectively.) You are working on the unit called "The City Environment." This chapter is about noise pollution. With your class write the paragraph for the textbook about the causes of noise pollution. Use the format for paragraphs about causes.
Topic Sentences: Define noise pollution and ask what the causes are.
Support: Support your topic sentence with information selected from your class discussion and from the causes that follow.

CAUSE AND RESULT I: Paragraphs

Cause	Examples	Approximate decibels
Industry	Equipment in factories, mines, construction	
Home	Air conditioners, record players, TV, radio, power appliances—lawn mower, vacuum, etc.	
Recreation	Boat motors, music from TV, records, etc., motorcycles, snowmobiles	
Transportation	Airplanes, buses, cars, trucks, motorcycles	

For the examples you choose try to give approximate decibel levels based on the scale on page 77.

Concluding Sentence: Write a statement which summarizes the content of the paragraph.

Exercise 3 Guided Writing

Do either A or B.

A. Write a paragraph about the causes of water pollution for the same science textbook (see Exercise 2). Use the format for writing paragraphs about causes.

Topic Sentence: Write a question asking about the causes of water pollution *or* write a sentence stating that several factors contribute to the pollution of our water.

Support: Support your topic sentence with some information from the chart below.

Causes of Water Pollution

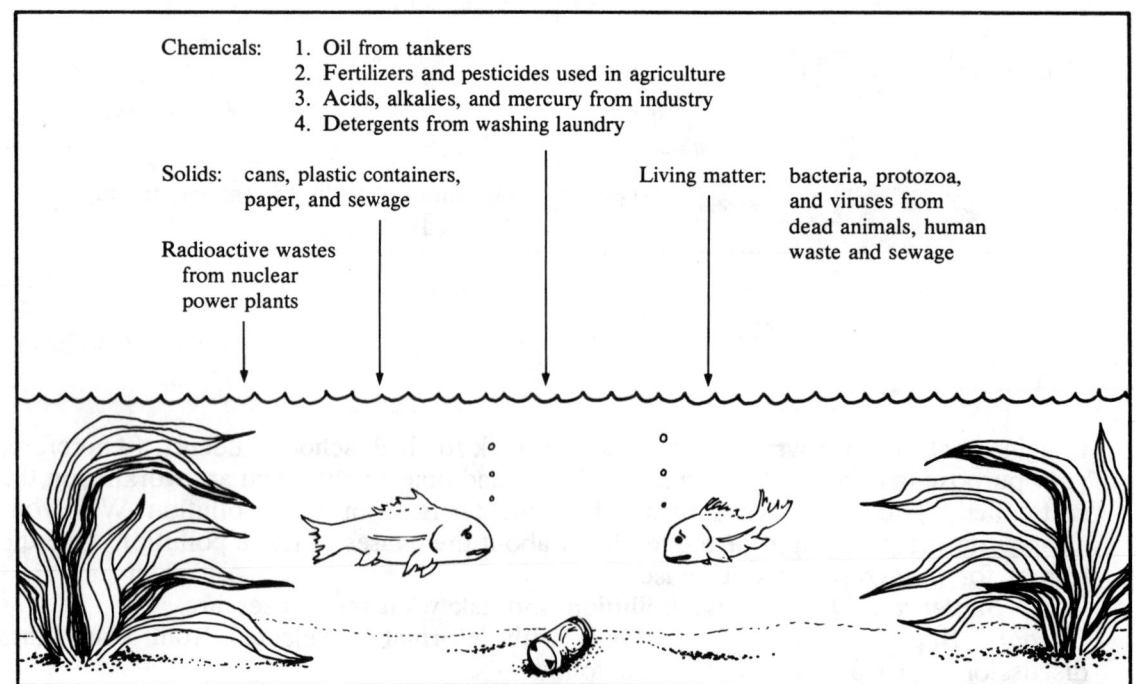

Chemicals:
1. Oil from tankers
2. Fertilizers and pesticides used in agriculture
3. Acids, alkalies, and mercury from industry
4. Detergents from washing laundry

Solids: cans, plastic containers, paper, and sewage

Radioactive wastes from nuclear power plants

Living matter: bacteria, protozoa, and viruses from dead animals, human waste and sewage

Concluding Sentence: Reformulate the topic sentence.

B. You are part of a team composing a textbook on European history for high school students. Your group is writing the unit about World War I: its causes, how it began, the major battles of 1914–1918, and the results. You are now planning the section about the causes. The first paragraph will introduce the major causes. Then each cause will be treated in greater detail. Write the paragraph which tells generally about the causes of the war. Use the format for writing paragraphs about causes.

Topic Sentence: State that there were a variety of causes of World War I.

Support: Support your topic sentence with the following information.

WORLD WAR I: CAUSES

1. Nationalism	Countries which were ruled by other nations wanted their own language and their own governments in their own land
2. Military alliances	Countries signed treaties with other countries for mutual protection against attack —
	The Triple Alliance: Germany, Austria, Hungary, and Italy
	The Triple Entente: France, Britain, and Russia
3. Secret diplomacy	Secret deals were made between nations
4. Competition for trade	There were many disagreements: arguments over new markets, control over new sources of raw material, new food sources, colonies and overseas bases

---

Concluding Sentence: State that in the following sections each cause will be examined more carefully.

Exercise 4   *Write Your Own Paragraph* (see Teacher's Notes, page 114)

Choose *one* of the following:

1. You are a writer for a television news program. A major political event has just occurred (an assassination, a riot, a military coup). Write the paragraph of your report which discusses the causes of this event.
2. A company is about to install computerized equipment. Many of the staff have become quite hostile. You were hired to interview the staff about their fears and to write about how to overcome the problem. Write the paragraph which explains the causes of the staff's hostility.
3. Write a paragraph for the student newspaper to explain the causes of a major problem or political event in your country/city/university.
4. Your choice. (Remember to decide on your audience and purpose.)

EXAM-TYPE QUESTIONS

Certain examination questions ask you to give causes of an event:

Briefly *give/explain* the *causes* of unemployment in the United States during the 1980s.

Your topic sentence should be a general statement using the key words from the question:

Several factors have caused unemployment in the United States during the 1980s.

Support your topic sentence with appropriate facts. Use discourse markers for expressing cause. Then conclude your paragraph with a sentence which summarizes the paragraph or restates the topic sentence.

Your teacher will give you practice with this type of question related to your reading or your own field of study.

8

CAUSE AND RESULT II: RESULTS

In this chapter you will learn how to write sentences and paragraphs which express result.

SENTENCES

Exercise 1

Work in groups. From the causes listed, select the one which is most interesting to you and your group. Then write the possible results of this cause in the spaces provided. (See Teacher's Notes, page 115.)

1. *Cause:* Your university has decided to double foreign students' fees.
   Results:

   a. _____

   b. _____

   c. _____

   d. _____

2. *Cause:* The air (or water) is polluted.
   Results:

   a. _____

   b. _____

   c. _____

   d. _____

3. *Cause:* People are exposed to a great deal of violence in all the media.
   Results:

   a. _____

   b. _____

   c. _____

   d. _____

82 CAUSE AND RESULT II: Sentences

4. *Cause:* Choose one of these (or other) 20th century inventions: the computer, the credit card.
   Results:

   a. _____

   b. _____

   c. _____

   d. _____

5. *Cause:* A cause whose results are of particular interest to you.
   Results:

   a. _____

   b. _____

   c. _____

   d. _____

**Discourse Markers for Expressing Result:
Group A**

Coordinator	Adverbial connectives
So	As a result Therefore Hence Consequently

Note: So is used in speech and informal writing. *Hence* and *consequently* are quite formal.

When the cause and result are in sentence form, use Group A discourse markers.

Exercise 2   Using Group A Discourse Markers

One class wrote the following for Exercise 1:

> *Cause*
> The university has decided to double foreign students' fees.
> *Results*
> Fewer foreign students will be able to study here.
> Only rich students will be able to come.
> Many students will have to go home without finishing their studies.
> Foreign students will go to other universities.

A *coordinator* or an *adverbial connective* can be used to link the cause and results.

Coordinator:
The university has decided to raise foreign students' fees *so* fewer foreign students will be able to study here.

Adverbial Connective:
The university has decided to raise foreign students' fees; *therefore*, fewer students will be able to study here.

1. Use Group A discourse markers to express two of the other results of raising foreign students' fees.

2. Now consider the results your teacher has written on the board from your work in Exercise 1. Write sentences using Group A discourse markers to express the cause and result relationship.

Discourse Markers for Expressing Result: Group B

Focus on result	Focus on cause and result
Nouns	Verbs and verb phrases
One/an/the effect One/a/the result } (of ___) One/a/the consequence	The result is after these: X { causes / results in / produces / leads to / brings about } Y The result is before these: Y { results from / is a result of / is caused by } X

Note: The cause (X) and the result (Y) are expressed in noun form. Often gerunds are used.

84 CAUSE AND RESULT II: Sentences

Exercise 3 Using Group B Discourse Markers

One class wrote the following effects of air pollution:

> *Cause*
> Air pollution
>
> *Effects*
> Damage to crops (fruit, tobacco, grain, vegetables)
> Damage to livestock (beef cattle)
> Deterioration of substances like metal, concrete, rubber, limestone, roofing
> Worsening of respiratory ailments (asthma, bronchitis, emphysema)

A. NOUNS   The nouns *effect, result,* and *consequence* can be used to write about the results of air pollution.

One *consequence* of air pollution is damage to crops.

1. Use the nouns *effect* and *result* to express two other results of air pollution.

   _____

   _____

2. Now consider the results your teacher has written on the board from your work in Exercise 1. Write sentences using *nouns* as discourse markers to express the cause and result relationship.

   _____

   _____

B. VERBS AND VERB PHRASES   You have already practiced using these in Chapter 7. If you want more practice, use these verbs and verb phrases to write about:
1. The effects of air pollution.
2. The effects you wrote about in Exercise 1.

Exercise 4 Sentence Combining

For each pair of sentences below, decide which is the cause and which the result. Combine the pairs of sentences using Group A discourse markers from both Chapter 7 (*because, since*) and this chapter (*so, as a result, therefore*). Punctuate carefully.
1. The professor threatened to fail the students. The students were noisy and belligerent in his class.
2. Supermarkets are introducing computerized scanning devices and omitting individual pricing for each item. Consumers are concerned.
3. The new model of their car had faulty brakes. The manufacturer recalled the cars.
4. Couples with more than two children are financially penalized. That country wants to limit population growth.
5. The students are planning a protest meeting. The cost of tuition is going to double.

CAUSE AND RESULT II: Sentences 85

Exercise 5 Writing Cause and Result Sentences

Work either alone, with a partner, or in groups.

A government committee is considering emphasizing the dangers of smoking by putting warnings such as the following on cigarette packages:

Warning: **Smoking may cause death from heart disease, cancer or emphysema.**

Write five warnings for submission to this committee. Use the information below and Group B discourse markers from this chapter. (Note the use of *may* in the example above to indicate possibility.)

Possible Effects of Smoking

Cancer of the lungs, mouth, respiratory tract
Chronic bronchitis
A higher probability of coronary heart disease
A greater likelihood of stomach ulcers
Smaller babies
Premature babies
Stillborn babies or miscarriages

1. _____
2. _____
3. _____
4. _____
5. _____

Exercise 6 Sentence Completion

Complete the following sentences using appropriate discourse markers from Chapter 7 and this chapter.

1. Rivers have become polluted. (result) _____

   _____

2. (cause) _____,

   the workers have gone on strike.

3. Universities are considering raising tuition fees for foreign students; (result) _____

   _____

86 CAUSE AND RESULT II: Sentences

4. The number of divorces is increasing in many countries. (result) _____

_____

5. (cause) _____ ,

   more women are working nowadays.

6. (cause) _____ ,

   there is a lot of violence.

Exercise 7 *Write Your Own Sentences*

Write cause and result sentences of your own. (Some possible topics are religion, unemployment, poverty, tension, nuclear armament, overpopulation, the feminist movement, etc.) Use appropriate discourse markers from Chapter 7 and this chapter.

1. _____

_____

2. _____

_____

3. _____

_____

4. _____

_____

5. _____

_____

PARAGRAPHS

Exercise 1 Read and Analyze

(1) It is not easy to tell when adolescents are taking drugs so parents and teachers must be aware of the effects. (2) One effect to watch for is a change in behavior. (3) For example, is there a change in school attendance (frequent lateness or absenteeism)? (4) Is there a change in work habits? (Is the adolescent's behavior sluggish and homework sloppy?) (5) Involvement with drugs may also produce unusual flare-ups, hyperactivity, aggressiveness, or sluggishness. (6) Drugs may cause dilated pupils, slurred speech, or poor muscular control. (7) If you suspect that a teenager is misusing drugs, contact a doctor or a counselor trained in dealing with drug abuse.

1. According to the topic sentence, what effects is the paragraph about?
2. Which effect is given in sentence 2?
3. What examples for this effect are given in sentences 3 and 4?
4. What emotional effects are mentioned in sentence 5?
5. Which physical effects are given in sentence 6?
6. What advice does the concluding sentence give?
7. Reread the paragraph. (*a*) Underline the discourse markers which express result. (*b*) Circle the discourse marker that introduces an example.
8. To avoid repetition of the words "taking drugs," the writer used different terms. What terms did he use in sentences 5, 6, and 7?
9a. For what audience was this paragraph written?
  b. Which of the following best describe the purposes of the paragraph: to inform, to request, to advise, to compare?

Format for Writing Paragraphs about Effects

Topic sentence(s): a question and/or statement which give(s) the cause for which you will discuss results

Support:
  Result plus example and/or explanation
  Result plus example and/or explanation } Appropriate discourse markers
  Result plus example and/or explanation

Concluding sentence: depending on the purpose of the paragraph, the concluding statement can be a summarizing statement, a reformulation of the topic sentence, a question, etc.

Exercise 2 Class Composition

1. Discuss this statement with your class or in groups: "The women's liberation movement has had effects on many different aspects of modern life." Write down the effects "women's lib" has had on women, men, families, the job market, the divorce rate, education, laws, etc.
2. Now consider the following information.

88 CAUSE AND RESULT II: Paragraphs

Some Facts and Figures about Women in Society

Work force: Women make up 37% of the labor force in the United States and 33% in Canada.

Professions: In the United States 7% of doctors are women, 3% of lawyers, and under 1% of engineers.
In Canada, 9% of doctors are women, 2% of lawyers, and under 1% of engineers.
In the U.S.S.R., 75% of doctors are women, 33% of lawyers, and 33% of engineers.

Laws: Various laws have been passed in many countries to ensure equal rights, equal pay, and lack of discrimination.

Education: More women are getting better educated. In the United States and Canada, 40% of college graduates are women. In schools, the emphasis is changing for girls; that is, before "women's jobs" were clerks, typists, nurses, teachers, and social workers. Now girls' education can have a broader scope.

Politics: Some women have entered politics and headed governments: in 1960, Sirimavo Bandaranaike of Sri Lanka became the first female prime minister. Later Indira Gandhi of India, Golda Meir of Israel, and Margaret Thatcher of England became heads of their governments.

---

3. Do either *a* or *b*.

a. With your class write a paragraph for the student newspaper about the effects of the women's liberation movement on society. Use the format for writing paragraphs about effects.

b. Work with a group of students from your own country or city and write a paragraph for the student newspaper about the effects of the women's liberation movement in your country/city. Use the format for writing paragraphs about effects.
Topic Sentence: State that in your opinion the women's liberation movement has affected society/your city or country.
Support: (*a*) Support your topic sentence with effects drawn from your discussion in question 1 and the fact sheet in question 2 or (*b*) support your topic sentence with specific effects from your knowledge of your own country/city.
Concluding Sentence: Reformulate the topic sentence or briefly summarize the content of the paragraph.

Exercise 3   Guided Writing

Do either A or B.

A. You are writing a science textbook for high school students. Write a paragraph which summarizes generally the effects of air pollution. Use the format for writing paragraphs about effects.
Topic Sentence: Write a question asking about the effects of air pollution on people and the environment or state that pollution of the air has serious effects on people and the environment.
Support: Support your topic sentence with information from the following chart and/or from your own knowledge.

CAUSE AND RESULT II: Paragraphs   89

Effects of Air Pollution

Health problems: Examples—respiratory ailments like asthma, bronchitis, emphysema.
Agricultural damage: Examples—in the United States, fruit, vegetables, grain, and tobacco crops are damaged. Beef cattle are affected.
Other effects: Many materials deteriorate more quickly. Example—steel surfaces wear away 30 times faster in a polluted city than in a rural unpolluted area.

Concluding Sentence: Write a summarizing statement or a reformulation of the topic sentence.

B. The town council is considering a motion to develop the town of Valleyford into a tourist center. For the next council meeting you have to write a report about the positive effects of this development.

Topic Sentence: State that you recommend the development of the town into a tourist center because it will have positive effects for the town and the people.

Support: Use the following notes to support your topic sentence.

> Notes for Council Meeting – Jan 9 – Positive Effects of Developing Valleyford
>
> - development → stimulation of the economy.
> - employment: more jobs in restaurants, hotels, stores, sports facilities.
> - more money will be available → residents will have money for schools, libraries, community centers.
> - tourist facilities (e.g., movies, theaters, concert halls, arenas) will benefit residents as well as tourists.
> - presence of tourists from all over the country → broadening of horizons for the residents.

Concluding Sentence: Write a summarizing statement or a reformulation of your topic sentence.

Exercise 4   Write Your Own Paragraph (see Teacher's Notes, page 116)

Choose *one* of the following.
1. The government has decided to dispose of nuclear wastes close to your town. You are very upset because the effects will be harmful. Write about these effects for the local paper.
2. You are a newsbroadcaster or newspaper reporter who writes political analyses. Write about the effects of an important political event in your country.
3. Invent a new drug and introduce it to doctors. Write the paragraph which tells about the positive effects of this drug.

4. Write a report for the town council in Exercise 3, Part B, about the negative effects of developing Valleyford into a tourist center.
5. Write your opinions for the student newspaper about *one* of the following: (*a*) effects of research into genetic engineering, (*b*) effects of computerizing processes in offices *or* industry, (*c*) effects of the continuing buildup of nuclear weapons.
6. Your own topic. (Decide on your audience and purpose.)

EXAM-TYPE QUESTIONS

Certain examination questions ask you to give results of an event. Such questions include the words *discuss, give,* or *explain* and words regarding results like *result, effect, consequence.*

"It is now generally believed that spraying insecticides is harmful to the environment." Discuss this statement by referring to the negative effects of insecticides.

Your topic sentence should be a general statement using the key words from the question.

The effects of insecticides are harmful.

Support your topic sentence with appropriate facts. Use discourse markers for expressing result. Then write a concluding sentence which reformulates the topic sentence or summarizes the paragraph.

Your teacher will give you practice with this type of question related to your reading or your field of study (see Teacher's Notes).

9

STATIC DESCRIPTION

Descriptions have a wide range of application. For example, companies write job descriptions for their employees and universities and colleges write descriptions of the courses they offer. You find descriptions of substances in science textbooks and descriptions of various items in magazines and newspapers. All these descriptions have a common denominator: they all describe in logical order the features of the item.

In this chapter you will learn how to write descriptive paragraphs of this kind.

Exercise 1 (see Teacher's Notes)

Work in pairs or in groups. Do either A or B.

A. Your friend has asked you to write him/her about the English course you are now taking. With your partner or group write down the information you would include in your description. Then compare the features/details you included with those of the other students in the class.

B. Write out a description of a famous person or of a person in your class, but *don't* use the person's name. Then read to the class what you wrote. See if the other students can guess the person you described.

Exercise 2 Read and Analyze (see Teacher's Notes)

Read the following paragraphs. As you read, consider the features that are described in each.

A. Description of a substance:

> The clove is a spice which comes from an Indonesian evergreen tree. Cloves are the dried, unopened buds of the tree. They are shaped like little nails. They are reddish when picked and turn dark brown when dried in preparation for use. Their fragrance is pleasant and strong and their taste is sharp and warm. This spice is used mainly in cooking and baking to heighten the flavor of foods such as fruit cakes and pies.

1. According to the definition in the topic sentence, what is a clove?
2. Fill in the features of cloves with information from the paragraph.

Shape _____

Color when picked _____

Color when dried _____

Smell _____

92 STATIC DESCRIPTION

   Taste _____

   Use _____

3. In which section of the newspaper do you think this descriptive paragraph appeared?

   Format for Paragraphs of Static Description
   Substance

   Topic sentence: a definition of the substance

   Support: description of the substance including relevant features from the following: size, shape, texture, taste, smell, color, flexibility, viscosity

   Concluding sentence: a statement about the significance, popularity, or major uses of the substance

B. Job description:

   The librarian for the children's section of the City Library will have a variety of responsibilities. Duties will include planning, organizing, implementing, and evaluating children's programs and services. The librarian will be responsible for building and maintaining the library's children's collection as well as supervising the staff of the children's section. The candidate for this position must have a bachelor's or master's of library science degree from an accredited library school and 3 to 5 years' professional experience. This person should enjoy working with children and should also be able to supervise adults. The salary will be commensurate with qualifications and experience.

1. According to the topic sentence, what position does this paragraph describe?
2. Fill in the spaces with information from the paragraph.

   Duties and responsibilities: _____

   _____

   _____

   _____

   _____

   Qualifications:
   a. _____

   b. _____

   c. _____

   Salary: _____

3a. For what audience was this job description written?
 b. For what purpose was it written?

> **Format for Writing Static Description**
> **Job Description**
>
> **Topic sentence:** a statement naming the job and the place of employment
>
> **Support:** duties and responsibilities
> qualifications (professional and personal)
>
> **Concluding sentence:** a statement about salary for the position

C. Course description:

> *Biology 100* is an introductory course for students who have little or no background in biology. The objective of the course is to give the student an understanding of basic concepts in biology. The course will include various aspects of cell biology, metabolism, and genetics as well as the evolution, structure, function, and ecology of living organisms. The course meets for 6 hours a week: 3 in lectures, 3 in the lab.

1. According to the topic sentence, (*a*) What course will the paragraph describe? (*b*) Which students is this course for?
2. Fill in the spaces with information from the paragraph.

Objective of the course: _____

_____

Content of the course: _____

_____

_____

Hours: _____

3*a*. For what audience was this course description written?
 b. For what purpose was it written?

> **Format for Writing Static Description**
> **Course Description**
>
> **Topic sentence:** states the name of the course and the people it is for
>
> **Support:** description of several of the following (as relevant): prerequisites, objectives of the course, content, hours, textbooks, cost of course, name of teacher, how and when to register
>
> **Concluding sentence:** this may be the last statement about the course— for example, how and when to register

Exercise 3 (see Teachers' Notes)

Discuss either in groups or with your class and teacher what features you would consider for a description of the following:

> A microcomputer
> A camera
> A (color) TV set
> An item of clothing (e.g., a coat)
> A smoke detector
> Other

Exercise 4 Class Composition

Work in groups. Imagine that you are opening a language school. Discuss the job description for "ideal" teachers for your school. Consider the responsibilities (teach, design curriculum, prepare materials and tests, etc.), the qualifications, both personal and professional, and the salary.

Now, with your teacher and class write a job description on the board.

Topic Sentence: State that the teachers for your school (give it a name) will be unique.
Support: Based on the discussions in your group, describe the major responsibilities and qualifications of the teachers.
Concluding Sentence: State what salary you will pay.

Exercise 5 Guided Writing

Do *one* of A. through E.

A. Based on the information below, write a description of the pineapple fruit for inclusion in an encyclopedia. Use the format for describing a substance. The definition will be your topic sentence and the uses the concluding sentence.

	PINEAPPLE
Definition:	A tropical plant which is known for its fragrant, juicy fruit
Shape:	Oval body with long, pointed sharp leaves on top
Outside:	Skin color—yellowish brown
	Skin texture—bumpy
	Leaves—dark green
Inside:	Flesh—white or yellowish white color, sweet tasting, soft texture
Use:	As a dessert, in salads, in casseroles

B. Based on the information on the next page, write a description of the heart for the same encyclopedia. Use the format for describing a substance. The definition will be your topic sentence and the significance your concluding sentence.

THE HEART
Definition: an organ of the body which pumps blood and carries oxygen to all parts of the body
Shape: conical
Position: behind lower breast bone. The apex touches the chest wall between the fourth and fifth ribs
Weight: 5/8 to 2/3 of 1% of a person's total body weight
Significance: if the heart stops beating and oxygen does not reach the brain and the rest of the body, the person will die
---

C. A head nurse is needed in the intensive care unit of the University Hospital. Use the following information to write an advertisement for the newspaper, describing the position.

HEAD NURSE—INTENSIVE CARE UNIT

Responsibilities: Planning, organizing, and directing all intensive care unit activities
Teaching staff and patients
Performing surgical, postoperative, and medical procedures

Qualifications: 3 to 5 years' experience in critical nursing
Registration with the State College of Nurses
Managerial skills

Interested Applicants: Apply to:
M. N. Smith
Director of Personnel
University Hospital
1 Belmont Avenue
392–2146

Topic Sentence: State the position available and the place where it is available.
Support: Describe the responsibilities and qualifications.
Concluding Sentence: Tell applicants how to apply for the job.

D. Write the job description for an advertisement for the following position with the City Broadcasting Network.

TRANSLATOR: ENGLISH/SPANISH

Responsibilities: Translation of administrative, commercial, and technical texts from English to Spanish
Revision of departmental and outside translations
Participation in terminology sessions with a group of peers

Qualifications: A degree in translation
2 to 3 years' experience
Ability to work under pressure of broadcast deadlines
Skills in working with a team

continued on page 96

96 STATIC DESCRIPTION

> *Salary:* $25,000 to $28,000
> Interested applicants apply in writing to:
> > Personnel
> > CBN News
> > P.O. Box 8748, Station F
> > Faircity, U.S.A.

Topic Sentence: State what position is available and with whom.
Support: Describe the responsibilities, qualifications, and salary.
Concluding Sentence: Tell candidates how to apply for the job.

E. You work for the Lieds Township Board of Education. Your job is to write descriptions of the continuing education courses offered by the board. Use the format for job descriptions and write a description of *either* 1 or 2 below.

1.
> CLERK-TYPIST COURSE
>
> For mature students who require secretarial/clerical skills
> Objectives of the course:
> > Develop typing speed and accuracy
> > Teach secretarial procedures
>
> Content of the course: dictatyping transcription from a dictating machine, accuracy development, business correspondence, filing, telephone techniques, and human relations skills
> Time: 8:30 A.M. to 12:30 P.M., Monday to Friday, May 10 to June 25
> Registration: in person at the Office of Continuing Education, Room 301, Administration Building

---

Topic Sentence: State the name of the course and the people it is for.
Support: Describe the objectives of the course, the content, and the time.
Concluding Sentence: Tell students how to register.

2.
> UNDERSTANDING COMPUTERS
>
> Objective: to improve managers' understanding of computers
> Course content: familiarization with the basic terminology of computers and computer systems; discussion of the advantages and disadvantages of computer systems in different management settings; evaluation of requirements and costs; basic programming; hardware, systems, and flowcharting
> Time: Monday and Tuesday 7:30 to 9:30 P.M., May and June
> Registration: in person at the Office of Continuing Education, Room 301, Administration Building

---

Topic Sentence: State the name of the course and the people it is for.
Support: Describe the objectives, course content, and time.
Concluding Sentence: Tell students how to register.

STATIC DESCRIPTION: Exam-type Questions   97

Exercise 6   Write Your Own Paragraph

Choose *one* of the following.

1. You have invented a new product (device or gadget) which you are introducing to the public. Write a paragraph to define and describe it. (Remember to mention its importance, usefulness, or ingenuity.)
2. Define and briefly describe a plant, fruit, or vegetable from your own country. (Select one which is unique or relatively unknown elsewhere.) Your purpose is to familiarize people with this item.
3. You are starting a new company (business, etc., of your choice). Write a concise job description for one of the key positions.
4. You are preparing the course list for your college (school, university). Write a short description of one of the courses.
5. Define and describe briefly *one* of the following:

    An organ of the body
    A mineral, liquid, or gas
    An unusual musical instrument
    A transistor

6. Your choice.

EXAM-TYPE QUESTIONS

Certain examination questions ask you for a description.

Describe hearing in insects.

The topic sentence for descriptive paragraphs is a general statement. The content of the statement will depend on the question. For the question above, the topic sentence could be:

Insects have a wide range of hearing, although many insects do not actually have ears.

The rest of the descriptive paragraph should support the topic sentence with a description of specific features. For this example, the features described would include the range of hearing, the organs of hearing (membrane vs. antennae), the position of the hearing organ, examples of specific insects with each type of hearing organ, etc. Conclude with a sentence which reformulates the topic sentence or summarizes the paragraph content.

Your teacher will give you practice with this kind of question relating to your reading or your own field of study.

10

CONSOLIDATION

Your task in this chapter is different from your tasks so far in this book. Here you are given information, an audience, and a purpose for your paragraph. You have to choose the most suitable organizational pattern. This task is similar to the one you will face when you have been given a written assignment: after researching your topic, taking notes, and selecting your data, you have to decide how to organize that data.

Exercise 1

A. In groups or as a class, discuss the information in numbers 1 through 9 and decide how you would organize the information for each paragraph.

B. Now work alone. Write paragraphs based on the information in numbers 1 through 9. For each paragraph use the kind of organization you discussed in A. Your teacher will tell you how many paragraphs to write.

1. You are a transportation consultant who has surveyed the Bay City Ferry System. Because of the increase in both passengers and vehicles carried in the past 10 years (1970–1980), you are going to recommend improvements to the system. Before writing about your recommendations, you have to prove that there has, indeed, been an increase in traffic. Use information from the two charts which follow as the basis of your paragraph.

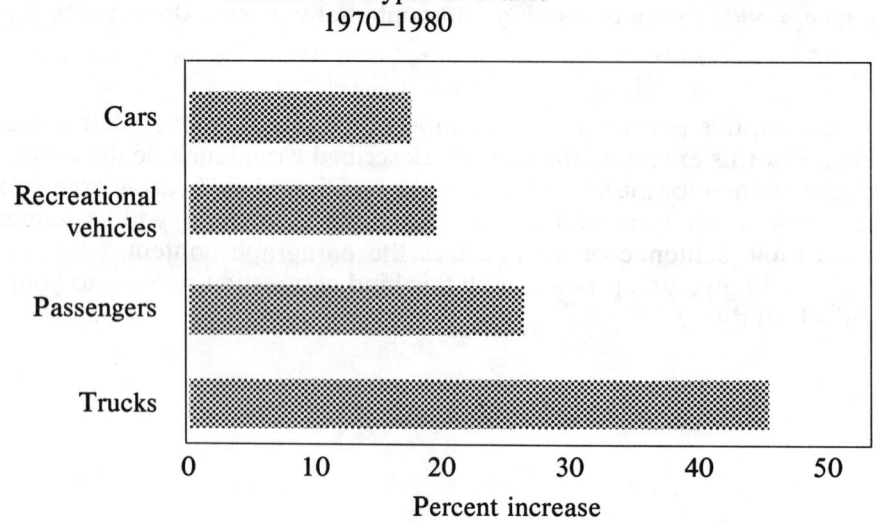

Bay City Ferry System:
Increase in Types of Traffic
1970–1980

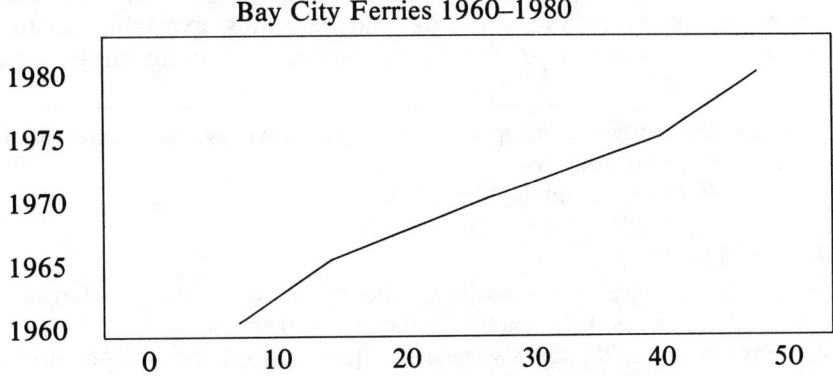

Number of Vehicles Carried on Bay City Ferries 1960–1980

2. You are the director of a senior citizens' home. The home requires a number of TV sets which the residents can either use in their rooms or take to the lounges. Your assistant has looked at many TV sets and narrowed the choices to the two described below.

Model	Price	Weight in pounds	Sound quality	Picture Quality		
				Clarity	Contrast	Freedom from distortion
Rolly 300	$110.00	13½	Good	Excellent	Acceptable	Good
Wyatt 301	$110.00	17	Acceptable	Good	Acceptable	Good

Decide which set you think the home should buy. Then write a short report (one paragraph) for the Finance Committee: recommend the model you chose and explain your selection by referring to the features of both sets in relation to the residents and their needs.

3. You are a doctor who writes a weekly newspaper column. You want people to use prescription and nonprescription drugs intelligently. This week's article is about aspirin. Use the information below to inform people about the positive aspects of aspirin and to warn them about the negative aspects.

ASPIRIN: some consider it a miracle drug

Reasonable use of aspirin:
    Pain relief, e.g., arthritic pain, backache, headache, toothache
    Lowering of fever
    Possible prevention of certain kinds of heart attack due to the anti-coagulant properties of aspirin

Excessive use of aspirin:
    Stomach upset
    Bleeding ulcer
    Death in children if too many aspirins are consumed

4. The university publishes a handbook at the beginning of each academic year to introduce new students to the services and facilities available to them. Use the information below to write a paragraph about the peer counseling center.

> Peer counseling center: a group of people your own age who offer advice, discussion, and guidance
> Place: Student Union Building, Room 200
> Hours: Monday–Friday, 9:00 A.M. to 6:00 P.M.
> Telephone: 238-6742
> Services offered: group discussions, individual counseling, referrals to specialists (if needed), career guidance, workshops
> Topics: nutrition, health, self-awareness, relating to others, birth control

5. You are writing the brochure which introduces to the public the new theater series at the City Playhouse. Use the notes below to write the paragraph which tells about the benefits of becoming a subscriber (i.e., of buying tickets for the series of five plays).

> Benefits of buying series tickets:
> 1. Save money—the subscription price is up to 25% below the cost of buying 5 single tickets
>   —subscribers can order tickets by mail for other performances at a 10% discount
> 2. Get the best seats—subscribers have first choice of seats
> 3. Receive advance information on other performances. Subscribers receive the Playhouse monthly calendar free

6. You write a monthly food column for a consumers' magazine. In your article you analyze trends in food prices and recommend what foods are most economical to buy.
    Read the following chart. Then, based on the information, write a paragraph about the trend in prices of produce, meat, and dairy products between January and February. Use the relevant facts from the chart to prove your statement about the trend.

	January	February
Steak (1 lb)	3.78	3.48
Chicken (3–4 lb)	1.55	1.39
Pork chops (1 lb)	2.59	2.49
Ground beef (1 lb)	2.28	2.18
Eggs (1 dozen large)	1.18	1.26
Milk (1 quart)	.74	.81
Butter (1 lb)	1.09	1.19
Bread (24 oz)	.71	.77
Fish (cod)	2.25	2.53
Potatoes (10 lb)	1.69	2.38
Tomatoes (1 lb)	.78	.98
Apples (1 lb)	.59	.68
Pears (28-oz can)	1.29	1.39
Peas (12 oz)	.61	.61
Coffee (1 lb)	4.12	3.49
Sugar (2 lb)	2.19	1.89

7. You are a newspaper reporter who is writing about a serious fire in a high-rise apartment building. The causes of the fire are unknown. Possibilities include the following:
   Carelessness (e.g., someone fell asleep while smoking in bed)
   Arson (there have been several apartment fires recently)
   A fault in the electrical wiring or a malfunctioning furnace
Based on the information above, write the paragraph about what may have started the fire.

8. Your friend, who lives in another city, has written asking for information and advice about the two universities in your city. He is an average student, with limited funds. He is a quiet person and prefers small places.
   Read the information below from the universities' calendars. Consider the size (number of departments), fees, language requirements, and standards (marks needed to achieve an A or first class honors). Then write your friend: tell him about the universities and suggest which you think is better for him.

HILSON UNIVERSITY

Departments
   Arts
   Social Science
   Journalism
   Commerce
   Public Administration
   Engineering
   Architecture
   Industrial Design
   Science
   Music

Fees
   Tuition: Arts, Commerce, Music, Journalism, and Science $600
   Engineering, Architecture, Industrial Design $680
   Miscellaneous: Students' Association, Athletics, Health Services $100

English requirements
   The instructional language of the university is English. Applicants must be able to understand and be understood in English, both written and oral. Proof of proficiency must be exhibited by a score of at least 550 on the TOEFL

Grades
   1st class   75% of over
   2nd class   61–74%
   Pass   51–60%
   Fail   below 50%

STATE UNIVERSITY

Departments
   Arts   Architecture
   Science   Industrial Design
   Commerce   Education
   Engineering   Dentistry
   Medicine   Agricultural Science
   Law   Social Sciences
   Nursing   Forestry
   Journalism

Fees (tuition plus student fees)
   Arts, Science, Commerce, Journalism, Education, Social Science, Architecture, Industrial Design, Engineering $900
   Medicine $964
   Dentistry $984
   Nursing $750
   Law $895
   Agricultural Science, Forestry $770

Grading
   A   85–100%
   B   76–84%
   C   70–75%
   D   61–69%
   Fail   under 60%

English requirements
   Applicants may be required to take a test in their own country to demonstrate facility in English. A score of 650 on the TOEFL is required for entrance to the university. Applicants whose English fluency is inadequate must take remedial English courses at their own expense

102 CONSOLIDATION

9. You are writing a pamphlet for distribution in dentists' offices to inform the adult patients about periodontal disease and to warn them about the dangers.

Read the notes below and decide (*a*) into how many paragraphs the information should be divided, (*b*) what organization to use for each paragraph.

Periodontal disease: A bacterial infection which attacks and destroys both the gum tissue and the bone around the teeth

Characteristics of the disease: It is painless.
   It is hard to detect.

Who is affected: People 35 years old and older, i.e., probably 90% of the over 35 population

Symptoms: Sore or tender gums
   Bleeding gums
   Swelling of the gums
   Loose teeth

Causes: Plaque—a sticky transparent substance which clings to the teeth and contains bacteria which attack the gum tissue and bone
   Poor nutrition and eating habits
   Lack of dental care
   Failure to clean teeth and gums properly

Results: Receding gums, infected bones, exposure of roots of teeth, destruction of the bone of the tooth socket, loosening of teeth, loss of teeth

---

TEACHER'S NOTES AND ANSWER KEY

CHAPTER 1—AN INTRODUCTION

This chapter introduces the student to the course. The first part presents the idea of functional relationships between sentences and the use of discourse markers to signal this relationship. The second part presents some major concerns of paragraph writing.

SENTENCES

Exercise 1

A. ADDITION
1. Very small computers are advantageous because they are portable *and* they use only small amounts of power.
2. Very small computers are advantageous because they are portable; *in addition*, they use only small amounts of power.

B. CONTRAST
1. Cigarettes are unhealthy *but* people continue to smoke.
2. *Although* cigarettes are unhealthy, people continue to smoke.
3. Cigarettes are unhealthy; *however*, people continue to smoke.

C. CAUSE/RESULT
1. The lake is polluted *so* the fish are dying.
2. *Because* the lake is polluted, the fish are dying.
3. The lake is polluted; *as a result*, the fish are dying.

Exercise 2

1. *Contrast*
   Overpopulation is becoming an increasingly serious problem but many families...
   Although overpopulation is becoming an increasingly serious problem, many families...
   Overpopulation is becoming an increasingly serious problem; however, many families...
2. *Addition*
   The government has limited the number of foreign students entering the country and universities have raised foreign student fees.
   The government has limited the number of foreign students entering the country; in addition, the universities have raised foreign student fees.
3. *Cause/Result*
   The workers' salaries weren't high enough so they decided to go on strike.
   Because the workers' salaries weren't high enough, they decided to go on strike.
   The workers' salaries weren't high enough; as a result, they decided to go on strike.
4. *Contrast*
   In the legends of North America the dragon is a threatening animal but in the tales of China...
   Although in the legends of North America the dragon is a threatening animal, in the tales of China...
   In the legends of North America the dragon is a threatening animal; however, in the tales of China...
5. *Cause/Result*
   TV sets have become cheaper to manufacture and sell so more people own sets.
   Because TV sets have become... sell, more people own sets.
   TV sets have become... sell; as a result, more people own sets.
6. *Addition*
   Some students try to cheat... answers and others cheat by writing... cuffs.
   Some students try to cheat... answers; in addition, others cheat by writing... cuffs.
7. *Contrast*
   Insects do not speak but certain insects, like bees... nectar is.
   Although insects do not speak, certain insects, like bees... nectar is.
   Insects do not speak; however, certain insects, like bees... nectar is.

Exercise 3

Some suggested methods of combining the sentences are given below.
1. *Addition and Cause/Result*
   The fathers were unemployed and the sons had no hope for their own future so they demonstrated angrily against the government.
2. *Contrast and Cause/Result*
   The space shuttle was ready to return to earth but the weather conditions... were poor. As a result, the descent was delayed twenty-four hours.
3. *Cause/Result and Addition*
   Because a woman is often paid less money than a man for doing the same job, women are becoming resentful and they are getting militant.

PARAGRAPHS

Exercise 1

1. Focus: nonverbal communication or ways of communicating that don't use language
2. Topic: book owners
   Focus: three kinds

3a. Focus: similarities (between the restaurants)
 b. Focus: differences (between the restaurants)
4a. Topic: anorexia nervosa
 b. Topic: anorexia nervosa
    Focus: causes

Exercise 2

1. Cries of warning and aggression, cries of contentment and affection, the dirty look, gestures (nod).
2. A person who has all the popular books but hasn't read them.
   A person who has many books, some of which he has read, most of which he has looked at, but all of which are clean.
   A person who has a few books or many, all of which are worn from continual use.
3. Similarities:
   Location
   Hanging plants
   Food—quiches, spinach salad, and carrot cake

   Differences:

	Copper Kettle	Pierre's
Age of customers	Young	(Older)
Food	Hamburgers	Gourmet
Music	Pop	Classical

4. Females between 12 and 18 suffer from anorexia
   Personality:
   Bright, sensitive
   She has high expectations and is self-critical
   Family:
   Upper-middle-class or rich
   Close with parents
   Parents are aware of weight and appearance and are concerned about athletics or fatness
   Parents have high expectations for their children—sometimes are overprotective or overinvolved
   Causes of anorexia:
   The need to feel in control of one's life
   Fear of growing up
   Family conflicts

Exercise 3

Paragraphs 1 and 2 and the second paragraph in 3 have concluding sentences.
The concluding sentence in paragraph 1 is a restatement. The concluding sentence in paragraph 2 is a summary. The concluding sentence in paragraph 3 is a recommendation.

Exercise 4

1. Topic sentence *b* is the best choice because it covers the ideas in the other sentences. *a* is too broad and is off topic because the importance of economics is not mentioned in the other sentences. *c* is too narrow. It mentions only two of the fields referred to in the other sentences.
2. The topic sentence should include the idea of the many different uses of small computers.
3. The topic sentence must include two elements:
   Caffeine is present in many substances
   Its presence is hidden (or we are often unaware of its presence)
   The concluding sentence could be in the form of a warning.
4. The topic sentence should mention that different kinds of pollutants exist everywhere.

Exercise 5

1. Each writer wants money.
2. The note is for the writer's mother. The memo is for the dean.
3. Differences:

	Note	Memo
Length	Short	Longer
Language	Colloquial (broke, help)	Formal [at the present time (vs. now), funds (vs. money)]
Person	First (I)	Third person (more formal and distant)
Explanations	No explanations	Three reasons given

4. *a.* Experts *b.* Laymen *c.* Experts

Exercise 6

Purpose	Vocabulary
Express cause	Because (of), since, on account of, etc.
Result	Therefore, as a result, consequently, etc.
Describe	
Remind, etc.	Remember, don't forget

Exercise 7

The journalist might include all the information.
The public health nurse could concentrate on Pregnancy (the section most relevant to expectant mothers) but might also include other effects on women.
Selection would depend on audience and purpose:

Purpose	Content
To fully inform	All the information
To warn	General health
To warn girls particularly	General health and Women

CHAPTER 2—MAKING/SUPPORTING GENERALIZATIONS

Discourse markers have been categorized in this text as follows:

Group A. Intersentential markers: coordinators, subordinators, and adverbial connectives are considered here. These words link sentences grammatically and also express the functional relationship between the sentences.

Group B. Intrasentential markers: other parts of speech (noun, verb, preposition, etc.) are included in this group. *Within their own sentences* these words have a grammatical role. They express a functional relationship between ideas in their sentence or with a preceding sentence.

In this chapter students learn about making generalizations. They do a survey, analyze the data, and make generalizations based on the data. They then learn to write paragraphs which support generalizations by examples and/or statistics. In addition, students practice narrowing down a topic so that its scope is feasible in a single paragraph.

The exam-type questions appear for the first time in Chapter 2. Students are shown how the organizational patterns taught in the chapter will help them answer certain types of exam questions.

SENTENCES

Exercise 1A

1. *a.* 17 *b.* 12 *c.* 5
   d. Connective: Generally speaking, the students preferred an exam to an evaluation.
   Determiner: Most/Many (of the) students preferred an exam...
2. *a.* 8 *b.* 6 *c.* 2
   d. Connective: On the whole, the A and B students preferred an exam...
   Determiner: Most of the A and B students preferred an exam...
3. *a.* 5 *b.* 2 *c.* 3
   d. Determiner: Some students preferred an exam; some preferred an evaluation.
4. *a.* 4 *b.* 4 *c.* 0
   d. Determiner: All (of the) students/Every student wanted an exam. None of the students wanted an evaluation.

Exercise 1B

On the whole, the C, D, and F students preferred an exam; two-thirds chose the exam and one-third chose the evaluation.

or

Many/Most of the C, D, and F students preferred an exam; 6 chose the exam and 3 chose the evaluation.

Exercise 5

1. Japan is a land of contrasts; for instance/example, graceful old temples ... buildings of concrete and steel.
2. Australia and England have some similarities. For example/instance, in both countries tea ... driving is on the left.
3. Most clerical jobs are held by women. For instance/example, in this country women do 80% of the clerical work.

Exercise 6

1*a.* Computers have entered many areas of our lives such as/like airlines, banks ... offices.
  b. Computers have entered many areas of our lives. Some examples are airlines, banks ... offices.
2*a.* There are many home remedies for the common cold such as/like hot milk or tea mixed ... whiskey.
  b. There are many home remedies for the common cold. Examples are hot milk or tea mixed ... whiskey.
3*a.* English language students have difficulty with the spelling and pronunciation of certain words such as/like *through*, *cough*, and *bough*.
  b. English language students ... words. (Three) examples are *through*, *cough*, and *bough*.

PARAGRAPHS

Exercise 1

A. 1. The topic is the increase in the percentage of women in the business world.
   2.

Year	Number or percent of women	Areas of business world
1971	4%	Masters of business administration
1980	19%	Masters of business administration
1970–1978	More than double	Management
	40%	Companies of 100 or more
	17%	Managerial and supervisory jobs

   3. On the whole
   4. The main clause (i.e., the doors to the business world are opening to women) refers to the topic sentence.
   5. Give information

B. 1. The topic is the difficulties of English for the writer.
   2.

Problem	Example and/or Explanation
Vocabulary	Examples: *thin, slender, skinny, slim* have similar meanings.
	Explanation: how do you know which to use?/It is difficult to know which to use.
Pronunciation	Examples: "th," "g," "k."
Writing	Examples: grammar, word order, and spelling.

3a. Generally speaking   b. Also; furthermore
c. Sentence 2—for example, sentence 3—like, sentence 6—such as
4. Synonyms for difficult—hard, for problem—obstacles, difficulties
   Note: It is useful to point out to students the stylistic value of using synonyms for a word instead of repeating it.
5. Express an opinion and explain it.

Exercise 2

The purpose of the class composition is to allow the teacher to guide the class as a whole in the first attempt at a paragraph written according to the suggested pattern. Discuss alternatives presented by the students so that it is clear that there are several ways to express the same idea.

Exercise 3

Discuss synonyms for "go up" which would be applicable for bank rates (increase, rise, soar, jump, etc.) and "go down" (drop, fall, dip, etc.).

Point out that discourse markers for contrast may also be used regarding the drop in rates in July and March.

Concluding sentence: Depending on their point of view, students might say that the bank rate could continue to rise, or it might stabilize, or it might fall because 19.5 is such a high rate.

If the writer were advising the public about investments and loans, he might advise the person who wants to borrow money to wait until rates were lower and the person who wants to invest money to do so since his money will be invested at a high rate of interest.

EXAM-TYPE QUESTIONS

In each chapter, the exam-type questions can be the link between this writing course and your students' reading course. The questions here and in Chapters 3 and 8, based on the article reprinted below, are given as examples of how to exploit reading material in order to elicit the writing of organized paragraphs.

NOISE POLLUTION CAN'T KILL—
IT CAN ONLY MAKE YOU DEAF, OR IRRITABLE, OR SICK[1]

Many studies in recent years have shown that it is not only working for long periods of time in noisy factories that causes deafness. Just living in a modern city can have an effect on our hearing and even short exposures to loud noises of over 90 dB can eventually cause deafness. Background noise in most North American cities is about 70 dB. Constant exposure to this noise level can cause what is known as partial deafness. This is a ringing in the ears that can last for 10 to 15 min. Sometimes the ringing is accompanied by a faster heart beat, dry mouth and stomach contractions. It is also thought, though this is still a controversial point, that noise can cause fatigue, ulcers, weight loss, high blood pressure and is a factor in nervous breakdowns.

Exposure to background city noise can also affect the learning ability of children. Recent tests have shown that children from similar socio-economic backgrounds living in the lower storeys of apartment buildings at busy intersections often have greater difficulty in learning to read than children on the higher floors or in high-rise buildings in quieter areas. This could be because in tuning out the background noise, the child also becomes less sensitive to nuances in speech sounds. Some children who have been thought to be slow learners, simply did not hear everything said in the classroom as they had become so used to tuning out sounds.

Noise does not only affect the ears. In many cases it has far worse effects on the nervous system. Sounds louder than 75 dB increase the pulse and respiration rate. According to one study, people working in areas of high-intensity sound tend to be more aggressive, distrustful and irritable than those working in quieter surroundings. Noise that interrupts sleep can be even more disruptive. If a person's dreams are interrupted night after night by sudden loud noises like a jet plane landing or taking off, he will become emotionally upset. One or two nights will not have much effect but it has been found that regular dreaming is essential for mental stability and constant interruption of dream sleep will cause nervous disorders. Surveys have shown that people living near an airport do have a significantly higher rate of admission to mental hospitals than people living in other parts of the city.

On the other side of the coin, noise can have some good effects. Regular or rhythmic noise can improve the speed people work at. Steady noise of up to 90 dB seems to make time pass faster. Some modern high-rise offices which shut out virtually all street noises are now introducing sound systems to keep workers alert and more efficient.

Steady noise is always more easily tolerated than sudden noises. People seem to sleep better if there is a heavy but regular flow of traffic outside than if there is only occasional noise like a passing train or an airplane taking off. Although it is possible to become accustomed to loud regular noise so that we think we hardly notice it any more, it can have hidden long-term effects on our ears, our ability to concentrate and our general health and nervous system.

One of the problems in dealing with noise pollution is that many people do not object to it. The idea that loud machines are more powerful and more efficient than quiet ones dies hard. There have been some cases where manufacturers have tried to market quieter appliances, but found that consumers are unwilling to buy them as they think they are less efficient. Another problem, of course, is that people enjoy noise. A rock concert, or even a symphony concert, can produce noise levels of over 90 dB and a day spent riding a snowmobile can cause hearing damage.

Even if we can't avoid noise completely, as least we can become more aware of it and of some of the harm it can cause. Perhaps eventually we will come to realize that noise does not mean power and that quiet is good.

For the "generalization" chapter, a task such as the following could be presented.

"Noise and behavior are related." Discuss this statement with reference to the article, "Noise Pollution Can't Kill—It Can Only Make You Deaf, or Irritable, or Sick."

The statement for discussion, or a version of it, becomes the topic sentence of the answer (i.e., the paragraph).

According to this article, noise and behavior are related.

or

This article indicates that noise and behavior are related.

Then the topic sentence is supported with the relevant facts from the article (i.e., only those facts relating noise to behavior, not to physical reactions, etc.). Appropriate discourse markers for examples and addition are used in the paragraph.

---

[1] Reprinted with permission of John Wiley & Sons Canada Ltd. from *From Nature to Man: Science and the Environment* by B. L. Barrett and J. N. Stratton, 1976.

TEACHER'S NOTES AND ANSWER KEY 109

According to this article, noise and behavior are related. *For instance*, studies were done which showed that noise influenced children's ability to learn to read. The children who lived in noisy surroundings blocked out the noise and apparently became less sensitive to subtleties of speech sounds as well. *Another example* of the relationship between noise and behavior is seen in the workplace. People who work where there is high-intensity sound tend to be "more aggressive, distrustful and irritable than those working in quieter surroundings." *On the other hand*, regular or rhythmic noise can improve people's work speed. *Finally*, if a person's sleep and dreams are interrupted night after night by sudden loud noises, he can become emotionally upset or suffer nervous disorders. *In short*, noise relates to behavior in both positive and negative ways.

CHAPTER 3—ENUMERATION

SENTENCES

Exercise 2

1. According to some, our survival on this planet is severely threatened. First, there is growing pollution. Second, population is increasing. Third, the nuclear arms race continues to escalate.
2. Teenage crime in this city can be reduced in two ways. First, increase the number of police officers on duty. Second, involve teenagers in meaningful activities.
3. There are several arguments for using industrial robots. First, they have high productivity. Second, they are reliable. Last/finally, they can do jobs dangerous or unhealthy for people.

Exercise 3

1. Nuclear reactions can occur by two different processes. One is nuclear fission; another is nuclear fusion.

   or

   The first is nuclear fission; the second is nuclear fusion.
2. According to one professor, there have been two changes in psychology in the past 15 years. The first/One change is a movement from a behavioristic to a cognitive approach. The second/Another is an increased interaction between psychology and other sciences which study people.
3. The teachers went on strike for three reasons. One/The first reason is higher wages. Another/The second is more preparation time. A third/The last is better working conditions.

PARAGRAPHS

Exercise 1

2. Topic—employees' main demands

Demands	Support
Higher wages	*Statistics:* cost of living increase—10%
Improved benefits	*Examples:* dental plan, higher vacation pay, pension plan
Better facilities	*Explanation:* cafeteria
Changes in work schedule	*Examples:* staggered hours, shorter shifts, longer breaks

   Concluding sentence—demands, strike
3. The first; the second (demand); the third (consideration); finally
4. Contrast: but
   Examples: such as, for example
5. Audience: (Mr. Smith), management of company
6. Purpose: inform management of the union's position and enumerate demands

EXAM-TYPE QUESTIONS

A question which would elicit a paragraph of enumeration based on the article on noise pollution on page 108 would read as follows:

List/Give **the main problems in dealing with noise pollution and briefly explain each.**

The students might write a paragraph like this:

There are *two* main problems in dealing with noise pollution. *First*, many people don't object to it. Many people think that if a machine is louder it is better. *Second*, many people enjoy noise. *For example*, people like rock music or snowmobile riding. Both of these activities produce sound of a high decibel level. These are two of the problems in handling or controlling noise pollution.

CHAPTER 4—COMPARISON I: TALKING ABOUT DIFFERENCES

SENTENCES

Exercise 2

1. The Lincoln is 5 miles from the university but The Kensington is only 1 mile away.
2. While The Lincoln is 5 miles from the university, The Kensington is only 1 mile away.
3. The Lincoln is 5 miles from the university; (however,) The Kensington (, however,) is only 1 mile away (, however).

Exercise 3

A. 1a. The Kensington is unlike The Lincoln.
    b. The Kensington differs from The Lincoln.
    c. The Kensington contrasts with The Lincoln.
    2. The Kensington is unlike/differs from/contrasts with The Lincoln regarding/with respect to size/age/distance from the university/number of appliances/rugs/carpeting.
B. 1. The Lincoln is bigger (larger) than The Kensington.
    2. The Kensington is older than The Lincoln.
    3. The Kensington is closer to the university. The Lincoln is farther from the university.
C. 1. Unlike The Kensington, The Lincoln has a balcony.
    2. Unlike The Kensington, The Lincoln has rugs.
    3. Unlike The Kensington, The Lincoln has a microwave oven and dishwasher.

Exercise 4

1a. Prince George students live at home but Queenstown students live at school.
    Prince George students live at home while Queenstown students live at school.
    Prince George students live at home; however, Queenstown students live at school.
b. Prince George School has boys and girls but Queenstown School has boys (only).
   Prince George School has boys and girls while Queenstown School has boys (only).
   Prince George School has boys and girls; however, Queenstown School has boys (only).
2a. Prince George School is larger than Queenstown School.
    Queenstown School is smaller than Prince George School.

or

In contrast to/Unlike Queenstown School, Prince George School is large.
Prince George is different from Queenstown School regarding/with respect to size.
One difference between Prince George School and Queenstown School is size.

b. The students at Prince George School are older than the students at Queenstown School.
   The students at Queenstown School are younger than the students at Prince George School.

Exercise 5

Some of the following:
1. *Comparatives:*
   The SX100 is smaller than the SX500.
   The SX500 is bigger than the SX100.
   The engine of the SX500 is bigger than the engine of the SX100.
   The SX100 gets more miles per gallon than the SX500.
   The SX100 is noisier than the SX500.
   The SX500 is more comfortable than the SX100.
   The SX100 needed fewer repairs than the SX500.

2. *Preposition:*

Unlike In contrast to	the SX100	the SX500	has is needed	4 doors. a 6-cylinder engine. moderately noisy. comfortable in both front and back. many repairs in the first year

3. *Verb:*

The SX100 differs from the SX500	regarding with respect to	size. number of miles per gallon. noise. comfort. repairs needed.

4. *Noun:*

One difference between the SX100 and the SX500 is	size. number of miles per gallon. noise. comfort. repairs needed.

TEACHER'S NOTES AND ANSWER KEY   111

5. The SX500 is comfortable in the front and the rear but the SX100 is comfortable only in the front.
    The SX100 required few repairs in the first year. However, the SX500 required many repairs.
    While the SX100 is very noisy, the SX500 is only moderately noisy.

PARAGRAPHS

Exercise 1 If necessary limit the number of topics so that there will be at least two students per topic.

A. In preparation for this exercise, survey your city for contrasting examples of restaurants, libraries (university vs. public library; university main library vs. departmental reading room), food stores, etc., or prepare lists of different makes or types of TV sets, cameras, tape recorders, etc.
   Then after students have chosen their area of interest and developed their bases of comparison, you can direct them toward specific places or items which will indeed lead to data for a paragraph of contrast.

B. Bases of comparison for hotels might include price, facilities at the hotel (dining room, snack bar, coffee shop, entertainment, swimming pool, games room, etc.), decor of rooms, size of rooms, service, atmosphere, size, etc.

Exercise 2

A. 2a. Sentence 1   b. Sentence 2
    3. The Varsity   4. The Towers
    5. On the other hand
    6a. Age, cleanliness, and condition; rent; facilities; children; and pets
     b. Same as above
     c. Same order
    7. Different; on the other hand; although; lower than; fewer; unlike; noisier
    8. (Therefore—not yet taught at this point in the book); so; as a result; as a result
    9. Both apartments are suitable for students. The amount of money they have (budget) and how they feel about noise (tolerance of noise) would affect apartment selection.
    10. The purpose is to contrast the two apartments and make a recommendation.

B. 1. Both apartments are considered in each.
       The bases of comparison are the following: sentence 3—age of apartment in relation to cleanliness and condition; sentence 4—rent; sentence 5—facilities; sentence 6—presence of children and pets in relation to noise in the apartments.
    2. Different; on the other hand; although; higher than; while; differ; quieter than
    3. Because the apartment is fifteen years old and starting to get run-down, there is an element of surprise that it is clean. *Although* is used to express this element of surprise.

Exercise 4

B. Be sure students pair up with students from countries whose educational systems differ. Otherwise, the data will yield a paragraph of similarity, not differences.

Exercise 5

Students may need your guidance if they choose numbers 2 or 3. The topics, as stated, are broad. Students will either have to narrow the topic down so that they are contrasting information that can fit into one paragraph (e.g., eating habits of two different insects), or they will have to write several paragraphs, contrasting different aspects of the topic (e.g., eating habits, the eyes, the body parts).

CHAPTER 5—COMPARISON II: TALKING ABOUT SIMILARITIES

SENTENCES

Exercise 2

The Kent is close to transportation. Similarly/Likewise, The Lionsgate has transportation nearby.

Exercise 3

A. 1a. The Lionsgate resembles The Kent—pattern 1.
    b. The Lionsgate and The Kent are similar—pattern 2.

2a.	The Lionsgate resembles The Kent regarding	furniture. washing machines.
b.	The Lionsgate and The Kent are similar with respect to	facilities. children and pets. charge for parking. lease. transportation. number of floors.

B. 1. Like The Lionsgate, The Kent has washing machines downstairs/in the basement.
   2. Like The Lionsgate, The Kent requires a 1-year/12-month lease.

C. 1. You might want to remind students here that the verb is plural after *both . . . and* and singular after *neither . . . nor.*
    a. Both The Lionsgate and The Kent have a pool, sauna, and party room.
    b. Both The Lionsgate and The Kent have 15 floors/stories.
   2a. Neither The Lionsgate nor The Kent allows/permits children.
    b. Neither The Lionsgate nor The Kent charges extra for parking.
       Note: The latter could also be expressed in this way: Both The Lionsgate and The Kent include parking in the rent.

112 TEACHER'S NOTES AND ANSWER KEY

Exercise 4

Some possibilities include the following:

1.	Model 2567 resembles / is similar to	Model 3000	regarding	weight. / the presence and absence of certain features.
2.	Model 2567 and Model 3000 are similar		with respect to	
3.	Like Model 2567, Model 3000 has		power control. / tone control.	
4.	Both Model 2567 and Model 3000 have		fast forward. / rewind.	
5.	Neither Model 2567 nor Model 3000 has		a tape counter. / a record meter. / a record light.	

PARAGRAPHS

Exercise 1

2a. Two housing possibilities
 b. The two places are alike.
3. Sentence 3—rent; sentence 4—size of room and furniture; sentence 5—condition; sentence 6—cooking and bathroom facilities.
4. Pattern 2
5. Alike; the same; both; both . . . and; neither . . . nor
6. His conclusion is that he cannot recommend the houses (because of their poor condition and inadequate amenities). He also believes that these houses should be removed from their list.
7. The purpose is to compare the two places (show similarities) and to make a recommendation.

Exercise 4

As in Write Your Own Paragraph in Chapter 4, you may have to guide your students so that they either limit their facts to one paragraph or write several paragraphs.

CHAPTER 6—DEFINITION

SENTENCES

As elsewhere, try to make this chapter as meaningful as possible for the student. Incorporate definitions that are relevant to your class.

Exercise 1

A. The aim here is to try to elicit from the students different ways of defining/explaining words both formally and informally. It becomes evident that some words are most easily explained by a synonym, some by actual explanations, and some by a formal definition; e.g., friendship is a relationship which exists between people who like each other.

 Neurotic—nervous or overly excited (informal) (synonym)

 Xenophobia—an irrational fear of strangers or foreigners (informal) (explanation)

 Use the suggested words or others more relevant to your class and try to elicit their meanings so that synonyms, explanations, and definitions are used.

B. Desalinization—a process which removes salt from sea water or saline water (formal)

 An alloy—a mixture of metals, especially a metal of low value mixed with a metal of high value (synonym)

 Calipers—an instrument which measures the diameter of round objects or the caliber of tubes (formal definition)

 A podiatrist—a person who is expert in treating problems of the feet (formal)

C. Some suggested definitions:
 1. I'm fed up—I've had enough of something (synonym)
 2. Uptight—very nervous or tense (synonym)
 3. Hung up—very neurotic (synonym)
 4. A numismatist is
   a person who collects coins and medals. (formal definition)
   a collector of coins and medals. (synonym)
 5. Anthropology is a science/subject which studies man, especially the beginnings, development, customs, and beliefs of mankind. (formal)

Exercise 2

1. Explanation in parentheses
2. Synonym—separated from the unknown word by a dash
3. Explanation introduced by "in other words"
4. Explanation introduced by "that is"
5. Synonym between dashes

Exercise 3

A. Commas, dashes, or parentheses could be used in all the sentences below.
 1. Manual laborers (people who work with their hands) often get very low wages.

2. Everyone would be annihilated—totally destroyed—in a nuclear war.
3. Some people don't have the capacity, the ability, to learn languages; others can't learn mathematics.
4. Neurotransmitters, brain chemicals like serotonin, carry messages between the nerve cells and the brain.

B. 1. Many children resemble their parents; that is,/in other words, they are like them in looks, personality, or behavior.
2. A person who goes without sleep for many days may become paranoic; that is,/in other words, he may think people are trying to harm him.
3. Some pills depress heart action and respiration; in other words,/that is, these pills reduce the rate of the heartbeat and of breathing.
4. Some governments are very hard on dissidents; that is,/in other words, they deal harshly with people who disagree with their policies.

Exercise 5

Class	Characteristics
1. An electrical appliance	Makes a liquid out of solid foods
2. A machine	Takes moisture out of the air
3. A red liquid	Flows throughout the bodies of humans and higher animals
4. A gadget	Used to remove a cork from a wine bottle
5. A sweet substance	Obtained from the juices of plants such as sugar cane or sugar beet

Exercise 7
1. An aviator is a person that/who controls an aircraft of some sort.
2. A choir is a group of people who/that are trained to sing together.
3. Astronomy is defined as a science which/that studies the sun, stars, moon, and planets.
4. A transistor is a small electronic device which/that is used in radios, hearing aids, computers, and other kinds of electronic apparatus.
5. The common cold is an infection which/that affects the nose, throat, air passages, and lungs.

Exercise 8
A. 1. Archaeology is the subject which is concerned with ancient things, especially remains of prehistoric times like ruins, tombs, and buried cities.
2. Evaporation is the process by which a liquid is changed to vapor.
3. An optician is a person who makes optical instruments, especially eyeglasses.
4. Oxygen is a gas without color, taste, or smell. It is present in the air and necessary for the existence of all forms of life.
5. A calculator is a machine that works automatically with numbers.

B. Stethoscope

CHAPTER 7—CAUSE AND RESULT I: CAUSES

SENTENCES

Exercises 1, 2, and 3

If the class works together, try to develop two cause/result relationships on the board: one in which the cause and result are in noun form, one in which they are in sentence form. For example:
Noun: gas fumes → air pollution
Sentence: people are unemployed → there is an increase in violence in cities.

If the class works in groups, circulate while students are writing and select two appropriate cause/result relationships for use as examples on the board: one in which the cause and result are in noun form, another in which they are in sentence form. Then demonstrate Group A discourse markers with the sentence example and Group B discourse markers with the noun examples.

Exercise 1
Some possibilities include the following:
1. *Result:* Air pollution
   Causes: *a.* Harmful substances from furnaces; *b.* Fluorocarbons in aerosol cans; *c.* Poisonous fumes from cars; *d.* Harmful particles from garbage incineration
2. *Result:* Insomnia
   Causes: *a.* Caffeine in tea, coffee, etc.; *b.* Stress or worry; *c.* Indigestion; *d.* Certain drugs
3. *Result:* There is an increase in violence in big cities
   Causes: *a.* Unemployment; *b.* Availability of weapons; *c.* Violence on TV, in films; *d.* Greater awareness of wrongs done by society
4. *Result:* People smoke although they know smoking is unhealthy.
   Causes: *a.* They don't think of consequences; *b.* They are addicted; *c.* They think smoking is sophisticated; *d.* They are obstinate

Exercise 3

In sentence A1 the result is stated in sentence form.

A1.

Because of Due to On account of As a result of	harmful substances from furnaces fluorocarbons in aerosol cans fine dust from grinding . . . processes evaporation of gasolines, paint, and solvents	the air is polluted.

B1.

One/A cause of air pollution is	harmful substances from furnaces, etc.

C1.

a.

Harmful substances from furnaces	cause result in lead to bring about produce	air pollution.

b.

Air pollution	results from is a result of is caused by	harmful substances from furnaces, etc.

Exercise 4

1. *Subordinator*
   a. Because/since divorce is becoming more acceptable, the divorce rate is increasing.
   b. Because/since many young people are not willing to stay in a marriage and try to make it work, there are more divorces now than there were before.
2. *Preposition*

a.

Because of Due to On account of As a result of	the relaxation of divorce laws,	more people apply for divorce.

b.

Because of On account of Due to As a result of	the reduction of the waiting period,	more people apply for divorces.

3. *Verbs and Verb Phrases*
   Note the verb tense—present perfect or past.

a.

Changes in divorce laws	(have) caused (have) resulted in (have) produced (have) led to (have) brought about	a rise in the divorce rate.

A rise in the divorce rate	(has) resulted from has been/was a result of was/has been caused by	changes in divorce laws.

b.

The availability of free legal services	(has) caused etc.	a rise in the divorce rate.

A rise in the divorce rate	(has) resulted from etc.	the availability of free legal services.

4. *Noun*
   Note: The students may need some guidance here in getting cause and result in the right order.
   a. A cause of the rise in the divorce rate is changes in divorce laws.
   b. A cause of the rise in the divorce rate is the availability of free legal services.

PARAGRAPHS

Exercise 1

1a. The causes of cancer
 b. There may be different causes for different forms of cancer, but no one knows for sure.
2. Cause 1: Working conditions
   Example 1—People who work with chemical compounds like arsenic or asbestos
   Example 2—People who work with x-rays or radioactive materials
   Kinds of cancer—leukemia, cancer of skin, bone, or lungs
   Cause 2: Smoking
   Kinds of cancer related: lung cancer; cancer of the mouth, larynx, esophagus, pancreas, and urinary bladder
   Cause 3: Viruses
   Explanation of research: certain viruses cause certain kinds of cancer in animals. Scientists are now investigating the validity of this discovery for humans.
4. Discourse markers for (*a*) cause—causes, lead to, cause, produce, cause, bring about, causes; (*b*) examples—for example; (*c*) enumeration—another, finally
5. Laymen
6. To give information about causes of cancer

CHAPTER 8—CAUSE AND RESULT II: RESULTS

SENTENCES

Exercise 1

As the students work in groups, check the work and choose examples for the board. Unless the class is sophisticated grammatically, select two sets of examples—cause and result in sentence form and cause and result in noun form. Then in Exercise 2, use the examples you selected to show how to use Group A discourse markers (coordinator and adverbial connectives) with the sentences and Group B discourse markers with the nouns.

If the class can handle sophisticated grammatical manipulation, one set of examples can be used:

| The university has raised tuition fees. | Fewer students will come to this school. |

Group A The university has raised tuition fees; as a result, fewer students will come to this school.

Group B a. The effect of doubling university fees is *that fewer students will come to this school.*
  b. The doubling of student fees will cause fewer students *to come* to this school.
  c. The doubling of student fees will lead to fewer students *coming* to this school.

Note: Sentence *a* requires a noun clause. Sentence *b* requires an infinitive construction. Sentence *c* requires a participial construction.

1. *Cause:* Your university has decided to double foreign students' fees.
Results
  a. Only rich students will be able to come.
  b. Many students will have to go home without finishing their studies.
  c. Foreign students will go to other universities.
  d. Foreign students will look for sources of funding (e.g., scholarships).
2. (a.) *Cause:* The air is polluted.
Results
  a. Worsening of respiratory ailments
  b. Damage to livestock
  c. Damage to crops
  d. Deterioration of substances like metals
  (b.) *Cause:* The water is polluted.
Results
  a. Fish die—Fishing industry affected; Balance of nature upset.
  b. Plants die.
  c. People get sick because of impurities in the water.
  d. Animals drinking polluted water suffer.
3. *Cause:* People are exposed to a great deal of violence in all the media.
Results
  a. They accept violence.
  b. They become immune to violence.
  c. They copy it.
  d. Children accept violence as a natural way of life.
4. (a.) *Cause:* The computer
Results
  a. (The) speeding up of many processes
  b. Greater efficiency in handling masses of information
  c. Loss of some jobs
  d. Creation of new jobs
  (b.) *Cause:* The credit card
Results
  a. People buy more.
  b. People pay more (in interest) for their items.
  c. People are encouraged to "overbuy."
  d. Development of new kinds of crime.

Exercise 2

1.	The university has decided to double foreign students' fees	so	only rich students will be able to come.
		; therefore,	many students will have to go home without finishing their studies.
		; consequently,	foreign students will go to other universities.

Exercise 3

1a.
| One A(n) | effect result | of air pollution | is | damage to livestock. deterioration of substances like metal. worsening of respiratory ailments. |

2a.
| Air pollution | causes results in produces leads to brings about | damage to crops. damage to livestock. deterioration of substances. worsening of respiratory ailments. |

b.
| Damage to crops Damage to livestock Deterioration of substances Worsening of respiratory ailments | results from is a result of is caused by | air pollution. |

TEACHER'S NOTES AND ANSWER KEY

Exercise 4

1. Because/Since the students were noisy ..., the professor threatened to fail the students.
   The students were noisy ...; as a result/therefore, the professor threatened to fail the students.
   The students were noisy ... so the professor threatened to fail them.
2. Because/Since supermarkets are introducing computerized scanning devices ..., consumers are concerned.
   Supermarkets are introducing ...; as a result/therefore, consumers are concerned.
   Supermarkets are introducing ... so consumers are concerned.
3. Because/Since the new model of their car had faulty brakes, the manufacturer recalled the cars.
   The new model of their car had faulty brakes; as a result/therefore, the manufacturer recalled the cars.
   The new model of their car had faulty brakes so the manufacturer recalled the cars.
4. Because/Since that country wants to limit population growth, couples with more than two children are financially penalized.
   That country wants to limit population growth; as a result/therefore, couples with more than two children are financially penalized.
   That country wants to limit population growth so couples with more than two children are financially penalized.
5. Because/Since the cost of tuition is going to double, the students are planning a protest meeting.
   The cost of tuition is going to double; as a result/therefore, the students are planning a protest meeting.
   The cost of tuition is going to double so the students are planning a protest meeting.

Exercise 5

Some of the following are possible:

A(n)/One effect result (of smoking) consequence	is	cancer of the lungs. chronic bronchitis. a higher probability of coronary disease.
Smoking	may cause may result in may produce may lead to may bring about	a greater likelihood of stomach ulcers. smaller babies. premature babies. stillborn babies or miscarriages.
Cancer of the lungs Chronic bronchitis etc.	may result from may be a result of may be caused by	smoking.

PARAGRAPHS

Exercise 1

1. Effects of taking drugs
2. Change in behavior
3. Change in school attendance and work habits
4. Unusual flare-ups (angry explosions), hyperactivity, aggressiveness, sluggishness
5. Dilated pupils, slurred speech, poor muscular control
6. Get help—doctor or counselor
7. (a) Result markers: sentence 1—so, the effects, sentence 2—one effect, sentence 5—may produce, sentence 6—may cause. (b) Example—sentence 3—for example
8. Sentence 5—involvement with drugs, sentence 6—drugs, sentence 7—misusing drugs
9a. Parents and teachers (people dealing with teenagers)
 b. Inform and advise

Exercise 4

Any of these topics could lead to compositions of several paragraphs. Either help students limit their information to single-paragraph scope or have them write several related paragraphs about effects.

EXAM-TYPE QUESTIONS

The following are two possible questions based on the article about noise pollution in Chapter 2.

Define noise pollution. Based on the article, "Noise Pollution Can't Kill ..." discuss the negative effects of noise.

or

By referring to the article, "Noise Pollution Can't Kill ..." discuss/give/explain some of the negative effects of noise.

The topic sentence of the answer restates key words from the question. For example, to answer question (b) a student could write the following:

Noise can have negative effects.

This sentence is supported by information about negative effects of noise from the article. Discourse markers for result are used. The concluding sentence summarizes what has been said in the paragraph.

Noise can have negative *effects*. It can *cause* partial or total deafness if people are exposed to high-intensity sound for long periods of time. *Due to* constant noise in their

TEACHER'S NOTES AND ANSWER KEY 117

environment, children's ability to read may suffer. High-intensity noise at work often *leads to* aggressive or irritable behavior among workers. *Also*, as a result of noise like jet planes which persistently interrupt sleep, people may develop nervous disorders. These are some of the negative aspects of noise.

CHAPTER 9—STATIC DESCRIPTION

The point to emphasize in this chapter is that whatever the subjects of the descriptive paragraph, there should be an orderly description of the features, properties, etc.

Since descriptive writing covers such a broad field, *choose only those examples in the exercises which are most relevant for the students in your class.* For example, if you have science students, select Part A in Exercise 2 (Read and Analyze) and numbers 1 or 2 in Exercise 5 (Guided Writing); in Exercise 6 (Write Your Own Paragraph) you could suggest descriptions of substances like copper, gold, blood, and carbon monoxide. Substitute topics so that the needs of your students are met; for instance, have hotel administrators write job descriptions or course descriptions appropriate for their field.

Remember: it is not necessary to work through all the models, guided writings, etc. Choose only those activities relevant for your class.

Exercise 1

The purpose of this activity is to show that this kind of writing involves description of features. Features to include for A—English course: number of hours; number of students; aims of course (e.g., speaking, writing); kinds of activity; cost; etc. Features to include for B—person: sex; country of origin; physical appearance—height, build, etc.; job, etc.

Exercise 2

Have students read and analyze only those descriptive paragraphs relevant to them. They don't have to work through all three paragraphs.
A. 1. A clove is a spice. It comes from an Indonesian evergreen tree.
   2. Shape—like little nails
       Color—when picked, reddish
       Color—when dried, dark brown
       Smell—pleasant and strong
       Taste—sharp and warm
       Use—in cooking and baking to heighten flavor
   3. Food section, consumer information, etc.
B. 1. Librarian for children's section of a library
   2. Duties and responsibilities: planning, organizing, implementing, and evaluating children's programs and services, supervising the staff. Qualifications:
       a. Bachelor's or master's of library science degree from an accredited library school
       b. 3 to 5 years' experience
       c. Enjoy working with children and be able to supervise adults
       Salary: commensurate with qualifications and experience
   3a. For potential librarians as a job advertisement
    b. For management as a guide in understanding exactly what this particular job entails
C. 1a. Biology 100
    b. Students with little or no background in biology
   2. Objective—to give students an understanding of basic biology
       Content—aspects of cell biology, metabolism, genetics, evaluation, structure, function, and ecology of living organisms
       Hours—6 hours a week (3 in lectures and 3 in lab)
   3. Students who want to take the course or perhaps as part of a letter to a potential teacher describing the course

Exercise 3

Microcomputer: Some features include the number of characters, the size of the memory, the language, printer, terminal (size, clarity), the keyboard, price, size, weight.

Camera: Some features are the quality of the picture (freedom from blur), the ease of adjustment, the weight, the shutter speed and range, the exposure control, view finder, and price.

(Color) TV Set: Some features include size of screen, weight, controls (e.g., color tuning), quality of picture, sound and color, price, warranty, convenience.

Item of Clothing (e.g., coat): Features include material, color, weight, warmth, style, price, practicality.

Smoke Detector: Features include the price, the type (photoelectric, ionization, or combination), the presence/absence of a pilot light, test button, and radioactive material, the effectiveness against smoke fires and flames, the loudness of alarm.

CHAPTER 10—CONSOLIDATION

Exercise 1

1. *Generalization Supported by Statistics:* When the students analyze the charts, be sure they note the dates required: 1970–1980. (The second chart has more information than they need.)
   There has been an increase in traffic generally.
   Chart 1. Increase in types of traffic 1970–1980: Cars increased 18%, recreational vehicles 20%, passengers 28%, and trucks 46%.
   Chart 2. Increase in number of vehicles carried on Bay City ferries between 1970 and 1980: In 1970, 26 million vehicles used the ferries, in 1975, 38 million, and in 1980, 46 million.
2. *Comparison:* The two sets are the same regarding price, picture contrast, and freedom from distortion. The differences are in weight (the lighter one, Rolly 300, would be better for senior citizens to carry around), sound quality, and picture clarity. The Rolly 300 rates better in both these areas—significant for senior citizens whose hearing or vision may not be good.
3. *Result:* There should also be the element of contrast between positive and negative effects. Suggest students introduce this contrast with an appropriate marker (however). If the students were to amplify the material given, they could write two paragraphs, one about positive effects and one about negative effects.
4. *Description*
5. *Enumeration*
6. *Generalization Supported by Examples/Statistics:* First, be sure students understand to which foods meat, produce, and dairy refer. Then have them compare prices and decide what the trend is. (They are not to consider bread, fish, coffee, and sugar.) On the whole, prices increased. This generalization should be supported by details from the chart. Discourse markers of contrast can be used (whereas in January milk cost $.74, in February it cost $.81). Since meat went down in price, a recommendation about stocking up on meat could be made.
7. *Cause*
8. *Contrast:* The universities are on the whole different.
   Size—State University is large, with more departments (students should give examples).
   Fees—State University is more expensive (students should give examples).
   Language requirements—State University has higher standards (650 on the TOEFL).
   Standards—State University requires higher marks (A = 85% and over. First class honors or A = 75% or over at Hilson).
   Given the friend's personality, abilities (average student), and finances, perhaps Hilson should be recommended.
9. The information could be divided several ways: (*a*) description: including definition, characteristics, who is affected and the symptoms; (*b*) causes; (*c*) results; or (*a*) description: definition, characteristics, who is affected; (*b*) enumeration: symptoms; (*c*) causes; (*d*) results.
   Help students to word a warning as a conclusion. The warning could be about recognition of symptoms or about seriousness of the results of the disease.